컴팩트 토익 스피킹

Compact TOEIC Speaking

IH-AL

북플레이트

컴팩트 토익 스피킹

초판 1쇄 발행 2025년 8월 29일
지은이   Joseph Ryu, (주)지알케이에듀케이션
펴낸곳   (주)에스제이더블유인터내셔널
펴낸이   양홍걸 이시원

주소   서울시 영등포구 영신로 166 시원스쿨
구입 문의 02)2014-8151
고객센터 02)6409-0878

ISBN 979-11-7550-000-6 13740

이 책은 저작권법에 따라 보호받는 저작물이므로 무단복제와 무단전재를 금합니다.
이 책 내용의 전부 또는 일부를 이용하려면 반드시
저작권자와 (주)에스제이더블유인터내셔널의 서면 동의를 받아야 합니다.

서문 Preface

○ 안녕하세요, 토익 스피킹 수험자 여러분!

오랜 준비 끝에 〈컴팩트 토익 스피킹〉을 선보이게 되어 무척 기쁩니다.

이 교재는 '갈수록 치열해지는 취업 경쟁 속에서 영어 자격 요건만큼은 부담 없이 갖출 수 있지 않을까?'라는 고민에서 시작되었습니다.

대부분의 한국인은 EFL(English as a Foreign Language; 외국어로서의 영어) 환경에서 영어를 접합니다. 이러한 환경에서 한국어와 뿌리부터 다른 영어를 모국어처럼 구사하기란 쉬운 일이 아닙니다. 수험자 여러분이 영어 실력을 향상하는 데 어려움을 겪고 있다면, 당연히 그럴 만하다는 말씀을 드리고 싶습니다.

그러나, 한 가지 희망적인 소식은 여러분이 도전하려는 토익 스피킹이 '시험'이라는 점입니다. 시험의 특성을 이해하고 그에 맞는 전략을 세워 학습하면, 여러분이 목표하는 바를 충분히 성취할 수 있을 것입니다. 그러니 자신을 의심하지 마시고 과감히 목표에 도전하시기를 바랍니다.

〈컴팩트 토익 스피킹〉은 현장에서 많은 수험생을 가르쳐 온 전문가들의 검토를 거쳐 제작되었습니다. 최신 토익 스피킹 출제 경향을 반영하였고, 출제 유형에 따른 효과적인 답변 방법을 담았습니다.

시험을 준비하고 계신 여러분께 이 책이 큰 힘이 되기를 바랍니다. 매일 조금씩 성장한다는 마음으로 꾸준히 연습하면 반드시 좋은 결과가 따를 것입니다. 모든 토익 스피킹 수험자 여러분의 도전을 진심으로 응원합니다.

○ Hello, TOEIC Speaking test-takers! We are excited to introduce <Compact TOEIC Speaking> to you after extensive preparation. With the job market competition in Korea becoming increasingly fierce, job seekers face a growing burden to enhance their qualifications, commonly known as 'resume building.' Therefore, this book was born out of the question, "Wouldn't it be possible for job seekers to obtain English qualifications, at least, without feeling overwhelmed?" The majority of Koreans learn English in an EFL environment. Learning a language distinct from their native tongue is not an easy task. However, here's some good news - the TOEIC Speaking test is an 'exam.' By understanding the test format and adopting appropriate study strategies, you can achieve your target score. So, have confidence in yourself and bravely take on the challenge. This book was made through a comprehensive review by experts who have instructed numerous test-takers. It addresses questions that reflect the latest trends in the actual TOEIC Speaking test, offering effective strategies for creating responses. We sincerely hope this book will be a valuable resource in your test preparation. With consistent practice, you will undoubtedly achieve favorable results. We wholeheartedly support all TOEIC Speaking test-takers in reaching their goals.

목차 Contents

- **교재 활용 가이드**
  - 교재 미리 보기
  Preview of this book
  - 맞춤 완성 학습 플랜
  Learning plan

- **TOEIC Speaking 공략 가이드**
  - 시험 소개
  All about TOEIC Speaking
  - 시험 진행 순서
  The order of exam

Chapter 1

- **PART 1**
  Read a text aloud 18
- **PART 2**
  Describe a picture 22
- **PART 3**
  Respond to questions 27
- **PART 4**
  Respond to questions using information provided 32
- **PART 5**
  Express an opinion 38
- **REVIEW TEST 1** 43

Chapter 2

- **PART 1**
  Read a text aloud 50
- **PART 2**
  Describe a picture 54
- **PART 3**
  Respond to questions 59
- **PART 4**
  Respond to questions using information provided 63
- **PART 5**
  Express an opinion 68
- **REVIEW TEST 2** 73

Chapter 3

PART 1
Read a text aloud 80

PART 2
Describe a picture 84

PART 3
Respond to questions 89

PART 4
Respond to questions using
information provided 93

PART 5
Express an opinion 98

REVIEW TEST 3 103

Chapter 5

PART 1
Read a text aloud 140

PART 2
Describe a picture 144

PART 3
Respond to questions 149

PART 4
Respond to questions using
information provided 153

PART 5
Express an opinion 159

REVIEW TEST 5 163

Chapter 4

PART 1
Read a text aloud 110

PART 2
Describe a picture 114

PART 3
Respond to questions 119

PART 4
Respond to questions using
information provided 123

PART 5
Express an opinion 128

REVIEW TEST 4 132

부록 Appendix

ACTUAL TEST 1 170

ACTUAL TEST 2 175

교재 미리 보기 Preview of this book

Groundwork 기초 다지기

각 파트의 출제 방식과 평가 기준에 따라, 고득점 달성을 위한 배경지식을 습득하고 자주 등장하는 문제 유형과 그에 맞는 답변 요령을 익힙니다.

Master The Basics 이론 학습

각 파트의 출제 유형을 이해하고, 채점 기준에 부합하기 위한 기초 지식을 학습합니다.

Type Analysis 유형 분석

파트별 빈출 주제와 그에 맞는 표현 및 답변 요령을 익힘으로써 출제 가능성이 높은 문제에 철저히 대비합니다.

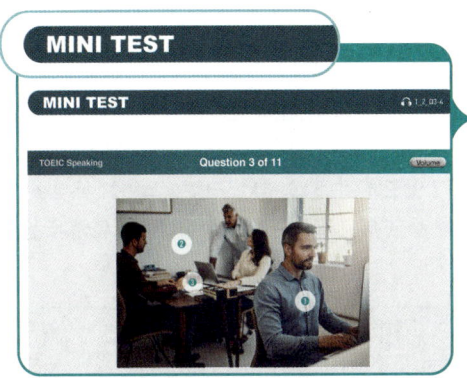

Mini Test 연습 문제

앞서 학습한 내용을 떠올리며 실전 난이도의 문제들을 풀어 보고 모범 답안을 확인하여 답변 실력을 탄탄하게 다져 나갑니다.

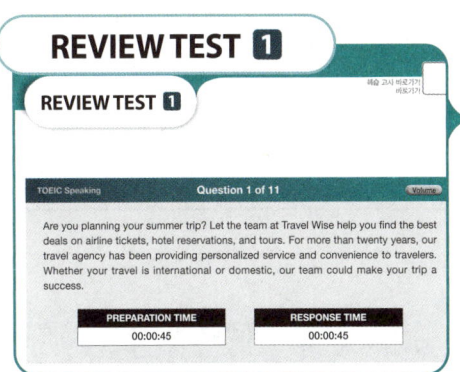

Review Test 복습 고사

파트 1부터 5까지 학습한 내용을 복기하며 실전에 임하는 자세로 복습 고사를 진행합니다.

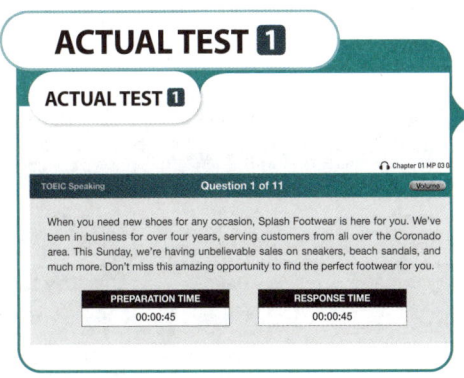

Actual Test 실전 모의고사

최신 토익 스피킹 출제 경향을 분석해 구성한 모의고사로, 시험 전 실전 모의고사를 풀어 보고 마지막으로 보완해야 할 부분을 확인합니다.

맞춤 완성 학습 플랜 Learning plan

📍 2주 완성 플랜　　　　　　　　　　　　　　　#단기 완성　#12일　#하루3단원

1. 단기간 준비하여 목표 등급을 얻고 싶은 수험자를 위한 학습 계획입니다. 토익 스피킹 응시 경험이 있는 분께 추천드립니다.
2. 하루 3개의 단원을 다루게 되므로, 학습한 내용이 휘발되지 않도록 기억해야 할 포인트를 필기해 두세요. 또한, 일일이 스크립트를 작성하는 것보다 자신의 답변을 녹음해 보고 이를 들으며 개선할 점들을 정리해 두는 편이 효율적입니다.

Day 1	Day 2	Day 3	Day 4	Day 5	Day 6
년　월　일	년　월　일	년　월　일	년　월　일	년　월　일	년　월　일
Chapter 1	Chapter 1	Chapter 2	Chapter 2	Chapter 3	Chapter 3
☐ Part 1	☐ Part 4	☐ Part 1	☐ Part 4	☐ Part 1	☐ Part 4
☐ Part 2	☐ Part 5	☐ Part 2	☐ Part 5	☐ Part 2	☐ Part 5
☐ Part 3	☐ Review Test 1	☐ Part 3	☐ Review Test 2	☐ Part 3	☐ Review Test 3
Day 7	**Day 8**	**Day 9**	**Day 10**	**Day 11**	**Day 12**
년　월　일	년　월　일	년　월　일	년　월　일	년　월　일	년　월　일
Chapter 4	Chapter 4	Chapter 5	Chapter 5	☐ Actual Test 1	☐ 주요 답변 요령 및 보완점 정리
☐ Part 1	☐ Part 4	☐ Part 1	☐ Part 4	☐ Actual Test 2	
☐ Part 2	☐ Part 5	☐ Part 2	☐ Part 5		
☐ Part 3	☐ Review Test 4	☐ Part 3	☐ Review Test 5		

📍 3주 완성 플랜　　　　　　　　　　　　　　　#꼼꼼 대비　#18일　#하루2단원

1. 꼼꼼히 대비하여 한 번에 목표 등급을 얻고 싶은 수험자를 위한 학습 계획입니다. 토익 스피킹을 처음 응시하시는 분께 추천드립니다.
2. 교재 구성을 순서대로 차근차근 학습해 보세요. 더불어, 각 단원의 <Mini Test> 구간을 통해 답변을 연습하고 자신의 답변을 모범 답안과 비교해 보세요. 자신의 답변과 모범 답안이 어떻게 다른지 분석하는 것만으로도 실력이 크게 성장할 수 있습니다.

Day 1	Day 2	Day 3	Day 4	Day 5	Day 6
년　월　일	년　월　일	년　월　일	년　월　일	년　월　일	년　월　일
Chapter 1	Chapter 1	Chapter 1	Chapter 2	Chapter 2	Chapter 2
☐ Part 1	☐ Part 3	☐ Part 5	☐ Part 1	☐ Part 3	☐ Part 5
☐ Part 2	☐ Part 4	☐ Review Test 1	☐ Part 2	☐ Part 4	☐ Review Test 2
Day 7	**Day 8**	**Day 9**	**Day 10**	**Day 11**	**Day 12**
년　월　일	년　월　일	년　월　일	년　월　일	년　월　일	년　월　일
Chapter 3	Chapter 3	Chapter 3	Chapter 4	Chapter 4	Chapter4
☐ Part 1	☐ Part 3	☐ Part 5	☐ Part 1	☐ Part 3	☐ Part 5
☐ Part 2	☐ Part 4	☐ Review Test 3	☐ Part 2	☐ Part 4	☐ Review Test 2

Day 13	Day 14	Day 15	Day 16	Day 17	Day 18
년 월 일	년 월 일	년 월 일	년 월 일	년 월 일	년 월 일
Chapter 5 ☐ Part 1 ☐ Part 2	Chapter 5 ☐ Part 3 ☐ Part 4	Chapter 5 ☐ Part 5 ☐ Review Test 5	☐ Actual Test 1	☐ Actual Test 2	☐ 주요 답변 요령 및 보완점 정리

📍 5주 완성 플랜   #부담 제로 #28일 #하루1단원

1. 기초부터 차근히 다져 목표 등급에 도달하고 싶은 수험생을 위한 학습 계획입니다. 영어 기초가 부족한 분께 추천드립니다.
2. 교재 내용을 꼼꼼히 살피고 자신의 것으로 소화해 보세요. 매일 한 단원을 학습한 뒤 중요한 포인트와 답변 아이디어를 체계적으로 정리해 놓으면, 시험 직전 참고하기 좋은 요약서가 만들어질 것입니다.

Day 1	Day 2	Day 3	Day 4	Day 5	Day 6
년 월 일	년 월 일	년 월 일	년 월 일	년 월 일	년 월 일
Chapter 1 ☐ Part 1	Chapter 1 ☐ Part 2	Chapter 1 ☐ Part 3	Chapter 1 ☐ Part 4	Chapter 1 ☐ Part 5 ☐ Review Test 2	Chapter 2 ☐ Part 1
Day 7	Day 8	Day 9	Day 10	Day 11	Day 12
년 월 일	년 월 일	년 월 일	년 월 일	년 월 일	년 월 일
Chapter 2 ☐ Part 2	Chapter 2 ☐ Part 3	Chapter 2 ☐ Part 4	Chapter 2 ☐ Part 5 ☐ Review Test 2	Chapter 3 ☐ Part 1	Chapter 3 ☐ Part 2
Day 13	Day 14	Day 15	Day 16	Day 17	Day 18
년 월 일	년 월 일	년 월 일	년 월 일	년 월 일	년 월 일
Chapter 3 ☐ Part 3	Chapter 3 ☐ Part 4	Chapter 3 ☐ Part 5 ☐ Review Test 3	Chapter 4 ☐ Part 1	Chapter 4 ☐ Part 2	Chapter 4 ☐ Part 3
Day 19	Day 20	Day 21	Day 22	Day 23	Day 24
년 월 일	년 월 일	년 월 일	년 월 일	년 월 일	년 월 일
Chapter 4 ☐ Part 4	Chapter 4 ☐ Part 5 ☐ Review Test 4	Chapter 5 ☐ Part 1	Chapter 5 ☐ Part 2	Chapter 5 ☐ Part 3	Chapter 5 ☐ Part 4
Day 25	Day 26	Day 27	Day 28		
년 월 일	년 월 일	년 월 일	년 월 일		
Chapter 5 ☐ Part 5 ☐ Review Test 5	☐ Actual Test 1	☐ Actual Test 2	☐ 주요 답변 요령 및 보완점 정리		

시험 소개 All about TOEIC Speaking

TOEIC Speaking이란?

- **문항 개수** 총 11문제
- **시험 구성** 5개의 파트로 구분되며, 파트별로 출제 유형이 다름
- **시험 시간** 약 20분
- **채점 기준** (1) 1점 단위로 점수가 매겨짐
  (2) 1~10번 문제는 0에서 3점, 11번 문제는 0에서 5점 범위 내에서 점수가 매겨지고,
      총점은 200점 만점을 기준으로 환산됨
  (3) 상대적으로 어려운 문항에 가산점이 적용됨

시험 구성

문제 번호	문제 유형	답변 준비 시간 (문항별)	답변 시간 (문항별)	채점 항목
1~2	PART1 : Read a text aloud 지문 소리 내어 읽기	45초	45초	발음, 억양, 강세
3~4	PART2 : Describe a picture 사진 묘사하기	45초	30초	발음, 억양, 강세, 문법, 어휘, 일관성
5~7	PART3 : Respond to questions 질문에 답하기	3초	5번: 15초 6번: 15초 7번: 30초	발음, 억양, 강세, 문법, 어휘, 일관성, 내용의 관련성, 내용의 완성도
8~10	PART4 : Respond to questions using information provided 주어진 자료를 활용하여 질문에 답하기	자료 분석: 45초 답변 준비: 3초	8번: 15초 9번: 15초 10번: 30초	
11	PART5 : Express an opinion 의견 제시하기	45초	60초	

☐ PART4의 경우, 8번 문제가 나오기 전 45초 간 화면의 자료를 분석할 시간이 주어집니다. 이후 8번 문제부터는 각 3초의 답변 준비 시간이 주어집니다.

등급 체계

☐ TOEIC Speaking 성적표에는 총점과 함께 ACTFL 등급이 제시됩니다.

등급	환산 점수	레벨 설명
AH Advanced High	200	• 업무와 관련된 긴 담화를 효과적으로 이끌어 나갈 수 있습니다. • 복잡한 요청에 대해 자신의 의사를 명확하게 전달할 수 있습니다. • 어법을 자유자재로 구사할 수 있으며 정확하고 세밀한 어휘를 사용할 수 있습니다. • 발음, 억양, 강세가 자연스러워 물 흐르는 듯한 의사소통이 가능합니다.

AM
Advanced Mid
	180~190	• 대부분의 경우 업무와 관련된 긴 담화를 이끌어 나갈 수 있습니다.
		• 복잡한 요청에 대해 자신의 의사를 효과적으로 전달할 수 있습니다.
		• 자연스러운 구어체를 구사하며 정확한 정보 전달이 가능합니다.
		• 발음이나 억양, 또는 복잡한 어법 구조를 사용함에 있어 사소한 오류가 발생할 수 있습니다.
		• 글을 읽을 때 발음, 억양, 강세가 자연스러워 청자가 낭독 내용을 쉽게 이해합니다.
		• 이 수준의 언어 사용자는 다음과 같은 기능을 수행할 수 있습니다.
		  - 토론이나 회의 중 자신의 의견을 말하고 강조할 수 있음
		  - 준비된 발표 자료를 읽거나 회의를 진행할 수 있음

AL
Advanced Low
	160~170	• 대부분의 경우 업무와 관련된 긴 담화를 이끌어 나갈 수 있습니다.
		• 복잡한 요청에 대해 자신의 의사를 효과적으로 전달할 수 있습니다.
		• 발음이나 억양, 또는 복잡한 어법 구조를 사용함에 있어 사소한 오류가 발생할 수 있으며, 머뭇거림이나 부정확한 어휘 사용이 있을 수 있습니다.
		• 글을 읽을 때 발음, 억양, 강세가 자연스러워 청자가 낭독 내용을 쉽게 이해합니다.
		• 이 수준의 언어 사용자는 다음과 같은 기능을 수행할 수 있습니다.
		  - 격식을 차려야 하는 상황에서 자신의 직책을 설명할 수 있음
		  - 발표나 연설에서 다루고 있는 주제에 대해 질문하거나 답할 수 있음
		  - 신규 입사자나 동료에게 사업 계획 또는 정책을 설명할 수 있음

IH
Intermediate High
	140~150	• 복잡한 요청에 대해 자신의 의사를 적절하게 표현할 수 있습니다.
		• 질의응답을 하거나 기본적인 정보 전달에 있어 크게 어려움을 느끼지 않으나 가끔 의사소통 오류가 발생할 수 있습니다.
		• 종종 발음, 억양, 강세, 어법 실수가 발생합니다.
		• 글을 읽을 때 청자가 낭독 내용을 잘 이해할 수 있습니다.
		• 이 수준의 언어 사용자는 다음과 같은 기능을 수행할 수 있습니다.
		  - 향후 목표에 대해 이야기할 수 있음
		  - 익숙한 업무 관련 절차를 묘사할 수 있음
		  - 회사의 연혁이나 내규를 설명할 수 있음

등급	환산 점수	레벨 설명

IM
Intermediate Mid
	110~130	• 대체로 자신의 의사를 표현할 수 있으나, 완벽한 문장을 구사하는 경우는 드뭅니다.
		• 같은 내용을 반복하여 말하는 경향이 있으며, 머뭇거림이 잦고 자신의 의사를 정확하게 전달하는 데 어려움을 느낄 수 있습니다.
		• 글을 읽을 때 청자가 낭독 내용을 대부분 이해할 수 있습니다.
		• 이 수준의 언어 사용자는 다음과 같은 기능을 수행할 수 있습니다.
		  - 일반적인 주제에 대한 담소를 나눌 수 있음 (e.g. 날씨)
		  - 외국인 방문객에게 짧은 관광을 시켜줄 수 있음
		  - 동료에게 일상적인 업무 수행 방법을 설명할 수 있음

IL
Intermediate Low
	90~100	• 의사를 표현할 수 있으나 대부분 짧거나 완전하지 못한 문장으로 발화합니다.
		• 어휘와 어법의 사용이 제한적이며 발음, 억양, 강세를 일관성 있게 구사하는 데 어려움을 느낍니다.
		• 머뭇거림이 잦은 편입니다.
		• 글을 읽을 때 글의 난이도에 따라 전달력 차이가 클 수 있습니다.
		• 이 수준의 언어 사용자는 다음과 같은 기능을 수행할 수 있습니다.
		  - 암기한 인사말을 건네거나 자기 소개를 할 수 있음
		  - 의견이 다른 상대방에게 자신의 의견을 말할 수 있음
		  - 가까운 역에서 익숙한 장소까지 가는 길을 간단한 수준으로 설명할 수 있음

NH
Novice High
	60~80	• 가까스로 의사를 표현할 수 있지만 근거를 들어 논리적으로 말하는 것은 어려워합니다.
		• 복잡한 요청에 대해 거의 대답하지 못합니다.
		• 간단한 설명을 할 때에도 제한적인 어휘와 어법을 사용합니다.
		• 글을 읽을 때 청자가 때때로 낭독 내용을 이해하기 어려워합니다.
		• 이 수준의 언어 사용자는 다음과 같은 기능을 수행할 수 있습니다.
		  - 암기한 인사말을 건네거나 자기 소개를 할 수 있음
		  - 의견이 다른 상대방에게 자신의 의견을 말할 수 있음
		  - 가까운 역에서 익숙한 장소까지 가는 길을 간단한 수준으로 설명할 수 있음

NM/NL
Novice Mid/
Novice Low
	0~50	• 의사를 표현하거나 근거를 말하는 것이 불가능합니다.
		• 복잡한 요청에 대해 대답하지 못하거나 관련 없는 답변을 합니다.
		• 일상적인 상황에서도 적절한 의사소통 수행이 불가능합니다.
		• 글을 읽을 때 청자가 낭독 내용을 이해하기 어려워합니다.
		• 이 수준의 언어 사용자는 다음과 같은 기능을 수행할 수 있습니다.
		  - 암기한 몇 가지의 단어로 자신을 소개할 수 있음
		  - 몸짓이나 손짓을 동원하여 손님에게 익숙한 인물, 사물, 또는 장소를 소개할 수 있음
		  - 카페나 식당에서 메뉴판을 활용하여 음식을 주문할 수 있음

응시 유의 사항

- **시험 접수**   온라인으로만 접수 가능하며, YBM 한국 토익 위원회 웹사이트(www.toeicswt.co.kr)에서 접수 일정 및 성적 발표일을 확인할 수 있습니다.
- **준 비 물**   규정 신분증
  * 수험표는 필수 준비물이 아니나 고사장 위치 등이 기재되어 있으므로 시험 전 반드시 확인하도록 합시다.
- **시험 당일**   (1) 시험 시작 후 10분이 지나면 입실이 금지되므로 미리 고사장에 도착하여 대기합니다.
  (2) 고사장 입구에서 본인의 이름과 수험 번호를 확인합니다.
  (3) 입실 후 감독관의 안내에 따라 오리엔테이션을 진행합니다.
  (4) 제공된 필기구로 OMR 카드를 작성합니다. 이때, OMR 카드 뒷면은 메모지로 활용할 수 있습니다.
     메모는 시험 시작 후부터 가능하므로 오리엔테이션 중 메모지를 사용하지 마세요.
  (5) 오리엔테이션 중 본인의 헤드셋과 마이크가 정상적으로 작동하는지 꼼꼼히 확인합니다.
  (6) 오리엔테이션이 끝난 후 감독관의 지시에 따라 본시험을 진행하세요.

시험 중 메모 꿀팁

 주어진 지문을 읽기만 하면 되는 유형이므로, 메모가 필요하지 않습니다.

 자신이 묘사할 대상과 그 내용을 키워드로 빠르게 메모해 두세요.

 이 파트에서는 답변 준비 시간이 불과 3초이므로, 메모를 권장하지 않습니다.

 답변할 내용보다 해당 파트에 자주 쓰이는 전치사 정도를 메모해 두는 것이 좋습니다.

 이 파트에서는 메모를 적극 권장합니다. 답변할 내용을 순서에 맞게 정리해 두면, 짜임새 있는 답변을 하는 데 도움이 될 것입니다.

* 위 내용을 반드시 지켜야 하는 것은 아닙니다. 본 교재에서 제공하는 메모 꿀팁과 실전 모의고사 등을 통해 본인에게 맞는 메모 방법을 찾을 수 있도록 합시다.

시험 진행 순서 The order of exam

오리엔테이션

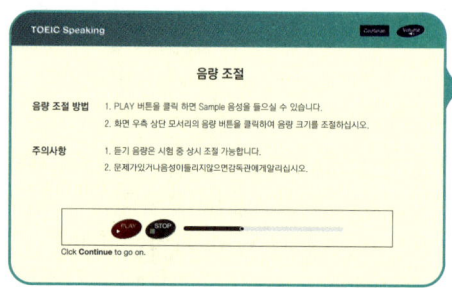

듣기 음량 테스트 화면
- 로그인 화면에서 본인의 생년월일과 수험 번호 입력
- 헤드셋을 착용하고 샘플 음원을 들어 보면서 본인에게 맞는 음량으로 조절

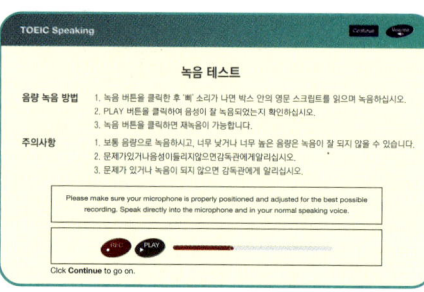

녹음 테스트 화면
- 화면의 지시에 따라 녹음 버튼을 누르고 주어진 문장을 소리 내어 읽기
- 녹음 후 재생 버튼을 눌러 답변이 잘 녹음되었는지 확인

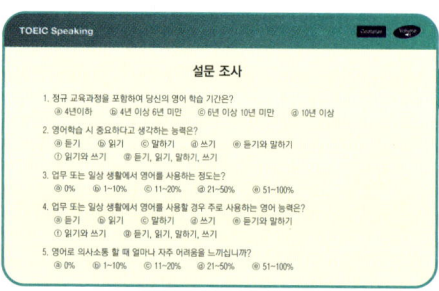

설문 조사 화면
- 응시자의 직업, 영어 학습 기간 등에 대한 설문 진행
- 문항 출제와 관련 없으므로 솔직하게 응답

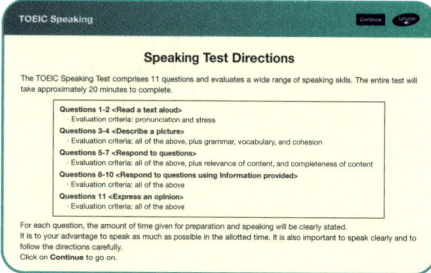

본시험 관련 안내 사항
- 화면을 통해 토익 스피킹 시험에 대한 전반적인 안내 사항 확인
- 우측 상단의 'Continue' 버튼을 누르면 본시험이 시작됨

본시험

Questions 1-2: Read a text aloud

Directions: In this part of the test, you will read aloud the text on the screen. You will have 45 seconds to prepare. Then you will have 45 seconds to read the text aloud.

파트별 디렉션 화면
- 각 파트가 시작되기 전 화면에 음성과 함께 제시
- 문제 유형과 준비 및 답변 시간에 대한 정보 확인

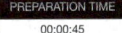

Join us this Friday at Bob's Home Appliances for our annual spring clearance sale. Customers will discover incredible savings on washing machines, dryers, and refrigerators. Most of our products will be marked fifty to seventy percent off. If you're considering getting something new for your home, come to Bob's Home Appliances this Friday because it's an opportunity you don't want to miss!

PREPARATION TIME
00:00:45

답변 준비 화면
- 화면에 문제가 등장
- "준비를 시작하라"는 음성과 함께 '삐' 소리 후 카운트다운

* PART4의 경우 문제가 나오기 전 자료를 분석하는 시간이 주어집니다.

Join us this Friday at Bob's Home Appliances for our annual spring clearance sale. Customers will discover incredible savings on washing machines, dryers, and refrigerators. Most of our products will be marked fifty to seventy percent off. If you're considering getting something new for your home, come to Bob's Home Appliances this Friday because it's an opportunity you don't want to miss!

RESPONSE TIME
00:00:45

답변 화면
- 화면 하단의 타이머가 "RESPONSE TIME"으로 변경됨
- "답변을 시작하라"는 음성과 함께 '삐' 소리 후 카운트다운

* PART4의 경우 문제가 화면에 표시되지 않으며, 음성으로만 제시됩니다.

Chapter 1

- **PART 1** Read a text aloud
- **PART 2** Describe a picture
- **PART 3** Respond to questions
- **PART 4** Respond to questions using information provided
- **PART 5** Express an opinion

REVIEW TEST 1

PART 1 Read a text aloud

GROUNDWORK

📍 Master The Basics 이론 학습

Background Knowledge 배경 지식

Read the following description and try to distinguish each pronunciation.
다음 설명을 읽고 각 발음을 구분해 보세요.

- **P vs. F** The 'P' sound is made with a sudden puffing of the air, almost resembling the movement of the mouth when one spits. The 'F' sound, on the other hand, is a continuous release of air between the top teeth and the bottom lip.
  e.g. pile-file, pail-fail, pull-full, pace-face

- **B vs. V** For the 'B' sound, the speaker has to block the air entirely with both lips and then release it. For the 'V' sound, the speaker has to place the top teeth gently on the lower lip and let the air pass through the gap between the teeth and lips.
  e.g. base-vase, berry-very, bet-vet, boat-vote

- **L vs. R** To produce the 'L' sound, the tip of the tongue presses against the insides of the top teeth. In order to make the 'R' sound, the tip of the tongue should not touch anything and rest somewhere in the middle further back.
  e.g. lane-rain, light-right, load-road, collect-correct

Practice 적용 연습

Read the given sentences aloud while paying attention to each pronunciation.
각 발음에 유의하여 주어진 문장을 소리 내 읽어 보세요.

- **P vs. F**
  - Can you pick up the phone for me, please?
  - Please fix your profile picture.
  - Do you prefer fax or phone?

- **B vs. V**
  - I love that berry bread very much.
  - The new vet is the best vet in town.
  - That's a very bad vase.

- **L vs. R**
  - I really love this road.
  - You have a leadership role for the job.
  - I will receive the lucky prize.

Type Analysis: Advertisement 유형 분석: 광고문

- Advertisement is one of the most frequently presented text types in PART 1.
- You will be in the position of the seller and promote a product, facility, or service.
- Try to get the intonation for list patterns such as "A, B, and/or C," in order to clearly communicate the perks of the product(s) you're trying to advertise.
- Don't forget to read the advertisement texts confidently.

Useful Expressions 유용한 표현

These are the vocabulary and expressions commonly found in the advertisement type texts of PART 1. Try to learn the meanings and pronunciations of each.
다음은 PART 1 지문 유형 중 광고문에 자주 쓰이는 어휘 및 표현들입니다. 각각의 뜻을 익혀 보세요.

• reasonable 합리적인	• clearance sale 정리 세일	• purchase 구매하다	• merchandise 물품, 상품
• experienced staff 숙련된 직원	• customer 고객	• savings 절약된 금액	• a wide selection of 다양한 ~
• price 가격	• delivery 배달	• opportunity 기회	
• discounted 할인된	• product 제품	• run out of ~이 바닥나다	
• popular 인기 있는	• make up 만들다, 구성하다	• affordable (가격이) 알맞은, 적당한	

Practice 적용 연습

Read the given passage with a bright and persuasive tone of voice while paying attention to the intonation marks.
억양 기호에 주의하며 다음 지문을 밝고 설득력 있는 어조로 읽어 보세요.

Are you searching for amazing Italian food at a reasonable price? ↗ Come by Etna's Restaurant located on Geary Avenue in the business district. We are well-known for our pizzas, ↗ pastas, ↗ and some of our authentic Italian dishes. ↘ For your convenience, we also offer takeout and delivery.

MINI TEST

🎧 C1 P1 Mini Test, 🎧 C1 P1 Model Answer

TOEIC Speaking　　　**Question 1 of 11**　　　Volume

Join us this Friday at Bob's Home Appliances for our annual spring clearance sale. Customers will discover incredible savings on washing machines, dryers, and refrigerators. Most of our products will be marked fifty to seventy percent off. If you're considering getting something new for your home, come to Bob's Home Appliances this Friday because it's an opportunity you don't want to miss!

PREPARATION TIME	RESPONSE TIME
00:00:45	00:00:45

Translation 해석

이번 주 금요일, Bob's Home Appliances에서 진행되는 연례 봄맞이 정리 세일을 저희와 함께하세요. 고객 여러분께서는 세탁기, 건조기, 그리고 냉장고 품목에서 굉장한 금액을 절약하실 수 있으실 겁니다. 대부분의 제품이 50~70% 할인되니, 가전 제품 구입을 고려 중이시라면, 이번 주 금요일 Bob's Home Appliances에 방문하세요. 놓칠 수 없는 기회니까요!

TOEIC Speaking   Question 2 of 11

Joy Cinema invites you to our year-end special for the month of December. On Wednesdays, all students receive discounted tickets, a free beverage, and a small-sized popcorn. On Fridays, all visitors will have the opportunity to win a prize of two movie tickets. If you want the best entertainment at an affordable price, Joy Cinema is the place for you!

PREPARATION TIME	RESPONSE TIME
00:00:45	00:00:45

Translation 해석

Joy Cinema에서 12월 한 달 간 진행되는 연말 이벤트에 여러분을 초대합니다. 매주 수요일, 모든 학생들에게는 티켓 할인, 무료 음료, 그리고 작은 사이즈의 팝콘이 제공됩니다. 매주 금요일엔 모든 방문객들에게 무료 관람표 2장의 상품 당첨 기회를 드릴 예정입니다. 합리적인 가격으로 최고의 엔터테인먼트를 원하신다면, Joy Cinema로 오세요!

PART 2 Describe a picture

GROUNDWORK

📍 Type Analysis: Office / Home 유형 분석: 사무실/집

Useful Expression 유용한 표현

These are the vocabulary and expressions that can be used when describing a picture taken in an office/home in PART 2. Try to learn the meanings and pronunciations of each.
다음은 PART 2 사진 유형 중 사무실/집에서 찍힌 사진을 묘사할 때 유용하게 쓸 수 있는 어휘 및 표현입니다. 각각의 뜻을 익혀 보세요.

- **office**
  사무실
- **meeting room**
  회의실
- **presenter**
  발표자
- **office supplies**
  사무용품
- **review**
  검토하다
- **discuss**
  ~에 대해 논의하다
- **concentrate on**
  ~에 집중하다
- **give a presentation**
  보고하다, 발표하다
- **take notes**
  메모를 하다
- **have a meeting**
  회의를 하다
- **kitchen**
  주방
- **living room**
  거실
- **kitchen utensils**
  주방용품
- **stove**
  가스레인지
- **look at**
  ~을 보다
- **be hanging on**
  ~에 걸려 있다

Sample Practice 예제 연습

Ideation

Look at the picture and think about what you want to focus on when describing it.
다음 사진을 보고, 무엇을 묘사할 것인지 생각해 보세요.

- Where do you think this picture was taken?
- What is the first thing you notice in this picture?
- What do you think the man standing at the front is doing?
- What are some things that are placed on the table?
- What do you see in the background of the picture?
- What do you feel when you look at the picture?

Answer Structure

Now, follow the steps below to organize your response systematically.
이제, 다음 순서에 따라 답변을 체계적으로 구성해 보세요.

STEP 1 — Place & Number of people

Begin by stating the location where the picture might have been taken and the number of people in the picture.

Pattern 1
This picture was taken in a(n) _____.
- office • conference room • meeting room

Pattern 2
I see _____ people in this picture.
- six • many

STEP 2 — Main person or thing

Describe the main person or thing in the picture.

Pattern
The first thing I'm noticing is a man/woman _____.
- giving a presentation • explaining something

STEP 3 — Surroundings

Say a few things about the rest of the picture by using location descriptions.

Pattern 1
In the middle of the picture, _____.
- I can see a big table • there are two vases

Pattern 2
I see _____ in this picture.
- two men in formal attire
- three people are sitting around the table

Pattern 3
In the background of the picture, _____.
- there is a glass wall of the conference room.

STEP 4 — Opinions or feelings about the picture

Conclude by expressing your thoughts or feelings about the picture.

Pattern 1
It seems like _____.
- a typical scene from a meeting room

Pattern 2
I like/don't like this picture because _____.
- it reminds me of my workplace

MINI TEST

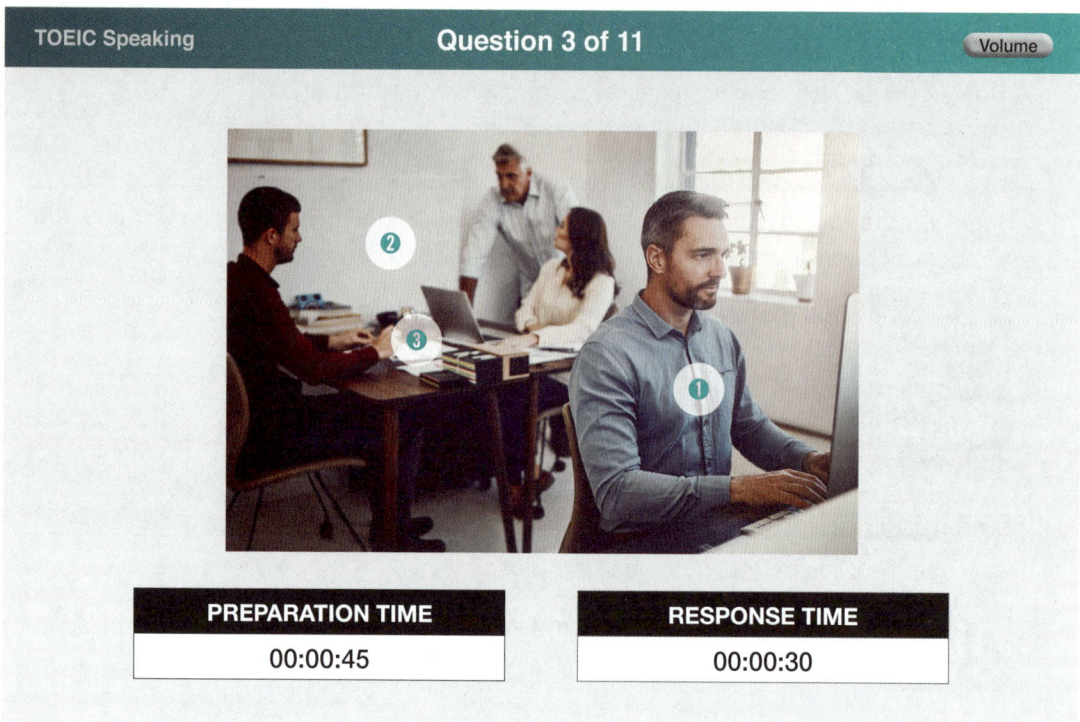

HINT 1 Answer Structure 답변 구조

This picture was taken in an office. I see four people in this picture.
❶ The first thing I notice is _____.
❷ In the background, _____.
❸ In front of _____, _____.
It seems like a typical office setting.

HINT 2 Useful Expression 유용한 표현

- blue shirt
  파란 셔츠
- have a discussion
  논의하다
- beard
  수염
- office supplies
  사무용품
- laptop
  노트북
- wooden table
  목재 책상
- concentrate on
  ~에 집중하다
- be placed on
  ~에 놓여 있다
- work on
  ~을 작업하다
- be hanging on
  ~에 걸려 있다
- document
  서류
- window
  창문

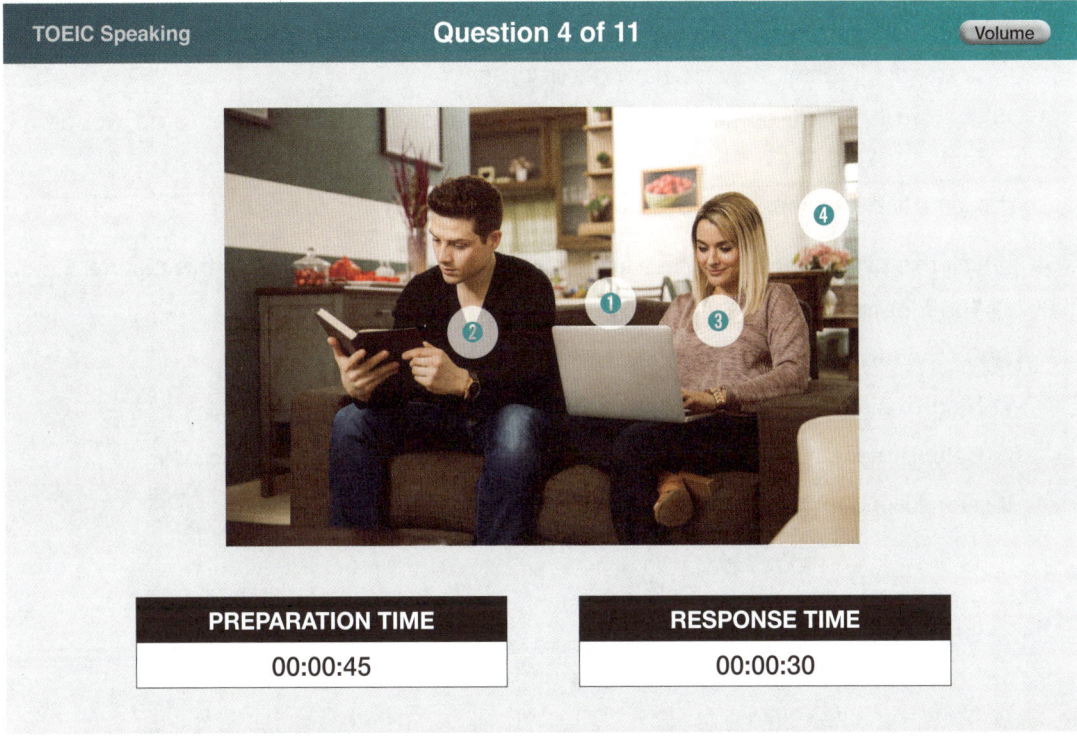

HINT 1 Answer Structure 답변 구조

I think this picture was taken in a living room. There are two people in this picture.

❶ The first thing I notice is _____.

❷ On the left, _____.

❸ Next to him, _____.

❹ Behind them, _____.

It seems like a married couple is enjoying their afternoon.

HINT 2 Useful Expression 유용한 표현

- living room
  거실
- kitchen table
  식탁
- sofa[couch]
  소파
- flower vase
  꽃병
- sit
  앉다
- be placed on
  ~에 놓여 있다
- read
  읽다
- married couple
  부부
- blond(e)
  금발(금발인 여자)
- enjoy
  즐기다
- type on one's laptop
  ~의 노트북으로 타자를 치다

Chapter 1 PART 2 Describe a picture 25

Model Answer 모범 답안

C1 P2 Model Answer

3. This picture was taken in an office. I see four people in this picture.

   ❶ **The first thing I notice is** a man working on a computer. He is wearing a blue shirt.

   ❷ **In the background,** I can see three people. Two people are sitting and one person is standing. I think they are having a discussion.

   ❸ **In front of** them, some office supplies and documents are placed on a wooden table.

   It seems like a typical office setting.

4. I think this picture was taken in a living room. There are two people in this picture.

   ❶ **The first thing I notice** is a man and a woman sitting on a sofa.

   ❷ **On the left,** a man in a black sweater is reading a book.

   ❸ **Next to him,** a blonde woman is typing something on her laptop.

   ❹ **Behind them,** I see a kitchen table and there is a flower vase placed on it.

   It seems like a married couple is enjoying their afternoon.

Translation 해석

3. 이 사진은 사무실에서 찍힌 사진입니다. 그리고 이 사진에서 네 사람을 볼 수 있습니다.

   ❶ **가장 먼저 눈에 띄는 것은** 컴퓨터 작업을 하는 남자입니다. 그는 파란색 셔츠를 입고 있습니다.

   ❷ **배경에는** 세 사람이 보입니다. 두 사람은 앉아 있고 한 사람은 서 있습니다. 그들을 논의를 하고 있는 것 같습니다.

   ❸ 그들 **앞에는** 사무용품과 문서들이 목재 책상 위에 놓여 있습니다.

   전형적인 사무실 풍경처럼 보입니다.

4. 이 사진은 거실에서 찍힌 것 같습니다. 이 사진에는 두 사람이 있습니다.

   ❶ **가장 먼저 눈에 띄는 것은** 소파에 앉아 있는 남자와 여자입니다.

   ❷ **왼쪽에는** 검은색 스웨터를 입은 남자가 책을 읽고 있습니다.

   ❸ **그의 옆에는** 금발의 여성이 노트북으로 타자를 치고 있습니다.

   ❹ **그들 뒤에는** 식탁이 보이고 그 위에 꽃병이 놓여 있습니다.

   한 부부가 오후를 즐기고 있는 것 같습니다.

PART 3 Respond to questions

GROUNDWORK

📍 Master The Basics 이론 학습

Background Knowledge 배경 지식

To answer the questions in PART 3, you need to understand what types of questions will appear on Question 5, 6, and 7 each.

PART 3에 출제되는 문제들에 답변하기 위해서는, 5번부터 7번까지 각 질문이 어떤 유형으로 출제되는지 이해할 필요가 있습니다.

Question 5, 6

Questions 5 and 6 are typically given in the interrogative form. Examples of the questions are as follows:

- How often ~? 얼마나 자주 ~?
- What kind of ~? 어떤 종류의 ~?
- How much money ~? 얼마 정도의 돈이 ~?
- When was the last time ~? 가장 마지막으로 ~한 것은 언제입니까?
- How many times ~? 몇 번이나 ~?
- On what occasions ~? 어떤 경우에 ~?

How to Answer

The most important thing is to begin with the key answer. Then you may add additional information such as reasons, feelings, etc.

Question: How often do you listen to music?
Answer: I listen to music every day. That's because it makes me feel happy.

Question: When was the last time you rode a bicycle?
Answer: I rode a bicycle three days ago. Riding a bicycle helps me reduce stress.

Question: How many meals do you usually have in a day?
Answer: I usually have two meals a day. I skip breakfast and just have lunch and dinner.

Tip

- key answer
- reused expression
- additional information

Question 7

Question 7 mostly asks for thoughts, opinions, choices, and pros and cons. Since you have to give a longer response than questions 5 and 6, make sure to provide more reasons or examples in your answer. Examples of the questions are as follows:

e.g.
- Do you prefer ~? ~을 선호하십니까?
- What are the advantages/disadvantages of ~? ~의 장/단점은 무엇입니까?
- What factors do you think ~? 어떤 요인이 ~하다고 생각하십니까?
- Would you ~? ~하시겠습니까?
- Which of the following do you think ~? 다음 중 무엇이 ~하다고 생각하십니까?
- Do you think ~? ~라고 생각하십니까?

How to Answer

The most important thing is to begin with the key answer. After that, provide additional information such as reasons, feelings, experiences, and so on. Remember to say as much as you can during the response time.

e.g.

Question: Do you prefer to watch movies at home or at the movie theater? Why?

Answer:
- **Topic sentence** I prefer to watch movies at home.
- **Time killer** I have a few reasons why.
- **Reason 1** First of all, it saves money. Watching movies at the theater can be expensive.
- **Reason 2** Also, I feel more comfortable at home. It's more relaxing.
- **Wrap up** So, I prefer to watch movies at home.

Question: What do you think are some advantages of having breakfast?

Answer:
- **Topic sentence** I think there are some advantages to having breakfast.
- **Time killer** I have a few reasons why.
- **Reason 1** Firstly, having breakfast is good for one's physical and mental health.
- **Reason 2** In addition, it helps me avoid feeling hungry in the morning, preventing me from binge eating at lunch.
- **Wrap up** These are some advantages of having breakfast.

Practice 적용 연습

Based on what you have learned, practice answering the frequently presented question types in PART 3.
학습한 내용을 바탕으로, PART 3에 자주 출제되는 질문 유형에 답변하는 연습을 해 보세요.

Question

1. **Question**: How often do you drink coffee?
   Answer: _____ drink coffee _____. That's because it gives me energy.

2. **Question**: Where do you usually purchase your clothes?
   Answer: _____ usually purchase _____ clothes _____. That's because it saves money and time.

3. **Question**: What kind of clothes do you usually wear when you go out with friends?
   Answer: I _____ when I go out with friends. That's because they are comfortable.

4. **Question**: What was the last book you read?
   Answer: _____. That's because _____.

5. **Question**: Do you prefer to work at home or at a café?
   Answer:
   - **Topic sentence**: I prefer to work _____.
   - **Time killer**: I have a few _____.
   - **Reason 1**: First of all, _____. I don't like to waste any time going back and forth to the café.
   - **Reason 2**: Also, because I _____ at home, I focus better.
   - **Wrap up**: So, _____.

Model Answer

1. I, everyday
2. I, my, online
3. usually wear a t-shirt and jeans
4. I read a sci-fi, it's fun and interesting
5.
   - **Topic sentence**: at home
   - **Time killer**: reasons why
   - **Reason 1**: working at home saves time
   - **Reason 2**: feel more comfortable
   - **Wrap up**: I prefer to work at home

MINI TEST

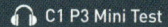
 C1 P3 Mini Test

TOEIC Speaking — Question 5 of 11 — Volume

Imagine that a US marketing firm is doing research in your country. You have agreed to participate in a telephone interview about riding bicycles.

When was the last time you rode a bicycle, and who did you ride with?

PREPARATION TIME	RESPONSE TIME
00:00:03	00:00:15

TOEIC Speaking — Question 6 of 11 — Volume

Imagine that a US marketing firm is doing research in your country. You have agreed to participate in a telephone interview about riding bicycles.

Where is a good place to ride a bicycle in your area?

PREPARATION TIME	RESPONSE TIME
00:00:03	00:00:15

TOEIC Speaking — Question 7 of 11 — Volume

Imagine that a US marketing firm is doing research in your country. You have agreed to participate in a telephone interview about riding bicycles.

Do you think riding a bicycle is good exercise? Why or why not?

PREPARATION TIME	RESPONSE TIME
00:00:03	00:00:30

Model Answer 모범 답안

5. The last time I rode a bicycle was two weeks ago, and I rode with my best friend Kevin. We had a great time.

6. A good place to ride a bicycle in my area is Central Park. It's only five minutes away from where I live, so I can save time.

7.
- **Topic sentence** — I think riding a bicycle is good exercise.
- **Time killer** — I have a few reasons why.
- **Reason 1** — First of all, I think it's good for my physical health.
- **Reason 2** — Also, it helps me relieve stress.
- **Wrap up** — That's why I think riding a bicycle is good exercise.

Translation 해석

상황 설정

미국의 한 마케팅 회사가 여러분의 국가에서 조사를 진행하고 있다고 가정해 봅시다. 여러분은 자전거를 타는 것에 대한 유선 설문 조사에 응하기로 했습니다.

5번 질문, 모범 답안

Q: 마지막으로 언제 자전거를 탔고, 누구와 탔습니까?

A: 마지막으로 자전거를 탄 것은 2주 전이고, 가장 친한 친구인 Kevin과 탔습니다. 우리는 즐거운 시간을 보냈습니다.

6번 질문, 모범 답안

Q: 당신이 사는 지역에서 자전거를 타기 좋은 장소는 어디입니까?

A: 제가 사는 지역에서 자전거를 타기 좋은 장소는 Central Park입니다. 저희 집에서 불과 5분 거리에 있어 시간을 절약할 수 있습니다.

7번 질문, 모범 답안

Q: 자전거 타기가 좋은 운동이라고 생각하십니까? 그 이유는 무엇인가요?

A:
- **Topic sentence** — 저는 자전거 타기가 좋은 운동이라고 생각합니다.
- **Time killer** — 몇 가지 이유가 있습니다.
- **Reason 1** — 우선, 신체적 건강에 좋은 것 같습니다.
- **Reason 2** — 또한, 스트레스 해소에도 도움이 됩니다.
- **Wrap up** — 그래서 저는 자전거 타기가 좋은 운동이라고 생각합니다.

PART 4 Respond to questions using information provided

GROUNDWORK

📍 Master The Basics 이론 학습

Background Knowledge 배경 지식

The questions in PART 4 will not appear on the screen during the test. Therefore, it is important to understand what types of questions are frequently presented in this part.

PART 4의 문제들은 음성으로만 제시되므로, 해당 파트에서 어떤 유형의 질문이 출제되는지 사전에 파악해 두는 것이 중요합니다.

Question 8

Question 8 is asked in the form of interrogative sentences. Questions related to date, location, starting time, and the first schedule are frequently asked. Also, two pieces of information are often asked at once.

e.g.

Question: Where and when will the conference be held?

Answer: The conference will be held on June 17 at the Kintex Conference Center.

Question: What is the date of the conference and what time will it start?

Answer: The conference will be held on June 17, and it will start at 10 a.m.

Question: What's the first item on the schedule and who is the presenter?

Answer: The first item is the keynote speech on the future of photography. The presenter is Zach Miller.

Question 9

Question 9 is presented in the form of a confirmation question. Most of the questions are asked to confirm information that the other party has misunderstood, or to give them updates on cancellations and postponements.

e.g.

Question: I heard that the demonstration will be in the morning. Is that right?

Answer: Actually, you have the wrong information. The demonstration will be held from 2 to 3 p.m. in the afternoon.

Question: I remember paying $15 to join the conference last year. It will be the same this year, right?

Answer: I am afraid that you have the wrong information. The fee is $25 this year.

Question: I have to bring my own lunch this year. Is that right?

Answer: Don't worry about that. Lunch is provided at the conference center cafeteria.

Question 10

Question 10 usually asks to list two items from the table. The most common format is to describe two overlapping items in the table in detail.

e.g.

Question: I'm especially looking forward to the workshops that you offer. Can you give me all the details about the workshops?

Answer: Sure. There are two scheduled workshops. First of all, from 1 to 2 p.m., a workshop on photography using smartphone technology will be held. It will be led by Yuko Sakamoto. Secondly, from 3 to 4 p.m., another workshop on photographing nature will be held. It will be led by Joseph Carter.

Question: I'm very interested in Sarah Hall's schedule. Could you give me the details of the sessions that Sarah Hall will be presenting?

Answer: Sure. There are two sessions led by Sarah Hall. First, from 11 a.m. to noon, a presentation on thinking in black and white will be led by her. Secondly, from 2 to 3 p.m., a demonstration on diverse perspectives will be led by her as well.

Question: Could you tell me the details of the sessions before lunch?

Answer: Sure. There are two items before lunch. First, from 10 to 11 a.m., a keynote speech on the future of photography will be held. And it will be given by Zach Miller. Second, from 11 a.m. to noon, a presentation on thinking in black and white will be held. It will be given by Sarah Hall.

Practice 적용 연습

Based on what you have learned, answer the following questions.
학습한 내용을 바탕으로, 다음 질문에 답변해 보세요.

Question

Spring Adult School
- Contra Costa Community Center -
Class term: March 2nd ~ May 13th

Day	Time	Class	Instructor
Mondays	9:00 a.m. ~ 11:00 a.m.	Fun Modern Dance Moves	Dan Sanford
	6:00 p.m. ~ 8:00 p.m.	Drawing (Basic)	Jenny Kim
Tuesdays	5:00 p.m. ~ 7:00 p.m.	Flower Arrangement	Becky Wolf
Wednesdays	10:00 a.m. ~ 11:30 a.m.	Cooking (Mexican)	Rick Perez
Wednesdays	3:00 p.m. ~ 5:30 p.m.	Latin Dance	Lorena Macias
Thursdays	6:00 p.m. ~ 7:30 p.m.	Hot Yoga	Kelly Brown
Fridays	2:00 p.m. ~ 3:30 p.m.	Swimming (Advanced)	Eddy Byers

1. Where do the classes take place? And what date does the class term start?
2. I think I saw the flower arrangement class listed on the schedule. The class will be held on Wednesdays, right?
3. I really like to dance. Could you give me the details on any dance classes that are being offered?

Model Answer

1. The classes will take place at the Contra Costa Community Center, and the class term will start on March 2nd.
2. I am afraid that you have the wrong information. The Flower Arrangement will be held on Tuesdays from 5 to 7 p.m.
3. Sure. There are two dance classes. First, the Fun Modern Dance Moves will be held on Mondays from 9 to 11 a.m. And it will be led by Dan Sanford. Also, Latin Dance class will be held on Wednesdays from 3 to 5:30 p.m. And it will be led by Lorena Macias.

MINI TEST

C1 P4 Mini Test

TOEIC Speaking — Question 8-10 of 11

La Jolla Interior Designers Conference
Brookview Hotel / Rose Hall
Sat, Oct. 2
Cost: $50

Time	Schedule	Presenter
9:00 a.m. ~ 9:30 a.m.	Registration and Refreshments	
9:30 a.m. ~ 10:30 a.m.	Keynote Speech: Dealing with Clients	Roger Goodwin
10:30 a.m. ~ 11:30 p.m.	Demonstration: Lighting Rooms Effectively	Hannah Chung
Noon ~ 1:00 p.m.	Lunch (Buffet / Hotel Restaurant)	
1:00 p.m. ~ 2:00 p.m.	Talk: Designing on a Small Budget	Jane Bagwell
2:00 p.m. ~ 3:00 p.m.	Demonstration: Choosing the Right Carpet	Jimmy Johnson
3:00 p.m. ~ 4:00 p.m.	Workshop: New Trends of Interior Design	Robert Mason

PREPARATION TIME
00:00:45

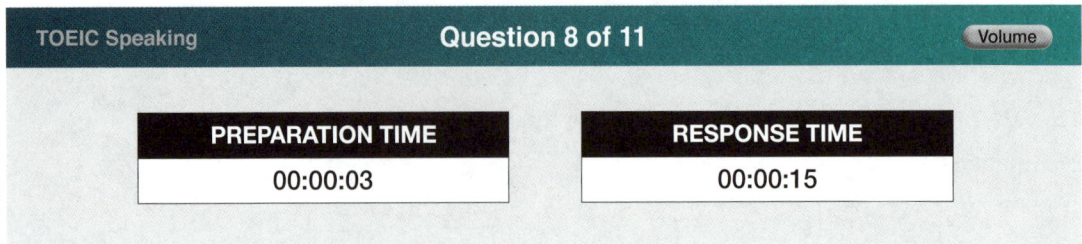

HINT Useful Expression 유용한 표현
- conference 학회, 회의
- registration 등록
- be held on ~에 개최되다
- begin(start) at ~에 시작되다
- Saturday 토요일

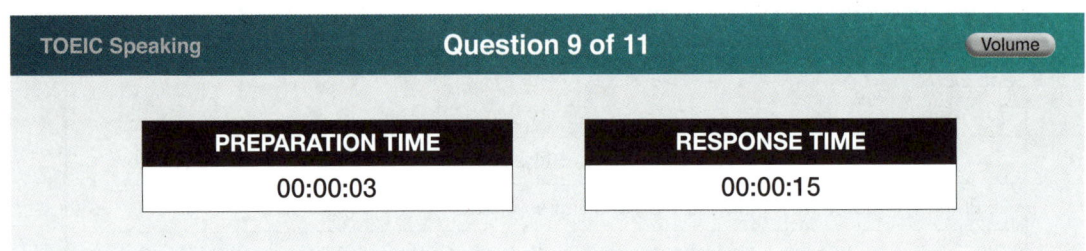

HINT Useful Expression 유용한 표현
- talk 연설, 강연
- be not the case 사실이 아니다
- I am afraid that … 유감이지만 …입니다
- from A to B A부터 B까지
- wrong information 잘못된 정보

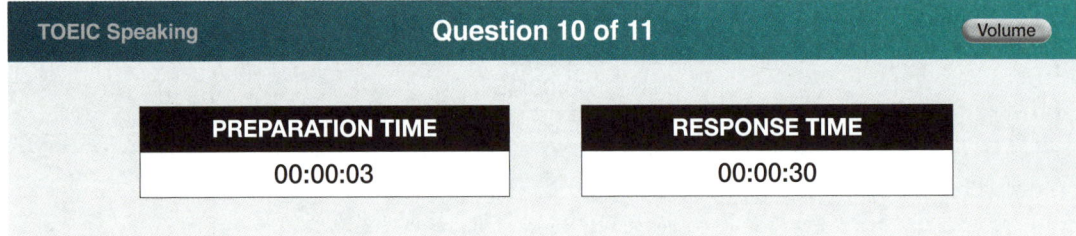

HINT Useful Expression 유용한 표현
- demonstration 설명, 시연
- First of all 먼저
- give the details 세부 사항을 알려주다
- Secondly 둘째로
- scheduled 예정된
- be presented [led] by ~에 의해 진행되다

Model Answer 모범 답안

🎧 C1 P4 Model Answer

La Jolla Interior Designers Conference
Brookview Hotel / Rose Hall
❽ *Sat, Oct. 2*
Cost: $50

Time	Schedule	Presenter
❽ 9:00 a.m. ~ 9:30 a.m.	Registration and Refreshments	
9:30 a.m. ~ 10:30 a.m.	Keynote Speech: Dealing with Clients	Roger Goodwin
❿ 10:30 a.m. ~ 11:30 p.m.	Demonstration: Lighting Rooms Effectively	Hannah Chung
Noon ~ 1:00 p.m.	Lunch (Buffet / Hotel Restaurant)	
❾ 1:00 p.m. ~ 2:00 p.m.	Talk: Designing on a Small Budget	Jane Bagwell
❿ 2:00 p.m. ~ 3:00 p.m.	Demonstration: Choosing the Right Carpet	Jimmy Johnson
3:00 p.m. ~ 4:00 p.m.	Workshop: New Trends of Interior Design	Robert Mason

Narration: Hello, I've received the time table for the La Jolla Designers Conference, but I seem to have lost it. I hope you can answer some questions for me.

8. Question: What is the date of the conference, and what time does registration begin?
   Answer: The conference will be held on Saturday, October second, and registration begins at 9 a.m.

9. Question: I heard that the talk by Jane Bagwell is in the morning. Is that right?
   Answer: Actually, you have the wrong information. The talk by Jane Bagwell will be held at 1 p.m. in the afternoon.

10. Question: I really enjoy the demonstrations at these conferences. Can you give me all the details about the demonstrations at the conference this year?
   Answer: Sure. There are two scheduled demonstrations. First, from 10:30 a.m. to 11:30 a.m., the demonstration on Lighting Rooms Effectively will be held. And it will be led by Hannah Chung. Second, from 2 p.m. to 3 p.m., the demonstration on Choosing the Right Carpet will be held. And it will be led by Jimmy Johnson.

Translation 해석

나레이션
안녕하세요, La Jolla Designers Conference 식순표를 받았었는데, 잃어버린 것 같아서요. 몇 가지 문의를 좀 해도 될까요?

8번 질문, 모범 답안
Q: 컨퍼런스 날짜는 언제인가요? 그리고 등록은 몇 시에 시작하나요?
A: 컨퍼런스는 10월 2일 토요일에 열릴 예정입니다. 그리고 등록은 오전 9시에 시작합니다.

9번 질문, 모범 답안
Q: 제가 듣기론 Jane Bagwell의 강연이 오전으로 알고 있는데요. 맞나요?
A: 사실, 잘못 알고 계십니다. Jane Bagwell의 강연은 오후 1시에 시작될 예정이에요.

10번 질문, 모범 답안
Q: 저는 컨퍼런스 시연회 가는 걸 좋아하는데요. 올해 컨퍼런스의 시연 관련 일정을 자세하게 알려주실 수 있나요?
A: 물론이죠. 두 번의 시연이 예정되어 있습니다. 첫째, 오전 10시 30분부터 11시 30분까지 '공간에 효과적으로 조명 쓰기' 시연이 예정되어 있습니다. 이는 Hannah Chung에 의해 진행될 예정입니다. 두 번째로, 오후 2시부터 3시까지 '딱 맞는 깔개 고르기' 시연이 예정되어 있습니다. Jimmy Johnson이 진행할 예정이고요.

PART 5
Express an opinion

GROUNDWORK

Type Analysis: Agree/Disagree 유형 분석: 동의/비동의 질문

Background Knowledge 배경 지식

The last question of the test may feel challenging to answer as it requires longer responses(60 seconds). Therefore, it is essential to understand the types of questions that are likely to be presented and practice how to structure your answers accordingly. We will now focus on the most frequently presented type of question, which is the "agree/disagree" question.

마지막 문제는 60초의 긴 답변을 요하기 때문에 까다롭게 느껴질 수 있습니다. 따라서, 문제 유형을 사전에 파악하여 유형별로 답변 구성을 연습하는 것이 중요합니다. 이번 단원에서는 가장 출제 가능성이 높은 '동의/비동의' 질문에 답변하는 연습을 해 봅시다.

Question Example

Do you agree or disagree with the following statement?

Technology has greatly improved our daily lives.

Give specific reasons and examples to support your opinion.

Answer Structure

Keep the following order in mind to respond to the question in a more organized manner.
다음 순서에 유념하여 답변을 논리적으로 구성해 보세요.

STEP 1 Determine your position

Repeat the expression in the question to explain your position.

| Expression to use | I agree/disagree that _____. |

e.g. I agree/disagree that technology has greatly improved our daily lives.

STEP 2 | Explain your reasons

Explain the reasons to back up your argument.

Expression to use
- The main reason is that _____.
- First of all, _____.
- Another reason is that _____.
- Additionally, _____.

e.g. First of all, you can access any information instantly with your smartphone.
Another reason is that technology and the internet can save you a lot of time.

STEP 3 | Support your reasons using examples

Use your own experience as an example to support your claims. It doesn't affect the score if the examples are not true.

Expression to use
- For example, _____.
- In my case, _____.
- To be more specific, _____.

e.g. For example, when you need help with your cooking, you can search for the recipe using your smartphone.
In my case, I don't go grocery shopping. I just order food and necessities using shopping applications.

STEP 4 | Conclude

Finish your response by summarizing the argument.

Expression to use
- Therefore, _____.
- For this(these) reason(s), I _____.
- That's why I _____.

e.g. Therefore, I believe technology has greatly improved our daily lives.
That's why I agree with the statement.

Chapter 1 PART 5 Express an opinion **39**

Practice 적용 연습

Based on what you have learned, answer the following questions.
학습한 내용을 바탕으로, 다음 질문에 답변해 보세요.

Question
Do you agree or disagree with the following statement?
It is easier to come up with creative new ideas when working in a group than when working alone.
Give specific reasons and examples to support your opinion.

HINT 1 Answer Structure 답변 구조

STEP 1 Determine your position
I _____ that it is easier to come up with creative new ideas when working in a group than when working alone.

STEP 2 Explain your reasons
- First of all, _____.
- Another reason is that _____.

STEP 3 Support your reasons using examples
- For example, _____.
- In my case, _____.

STEP 4 Conclude
Therefore, I _____ with the statement.

HINT 2 Useful Expression 유용한 표현

- share ideas 아이디어를 공유하다
- come up with ~을 생각해 내다
- productivity 생산성
- team player 팀으로 활동하는 사람
- save time 시간을 아끼다
- accomplish 성취하다
- focus on ~에 집중하다
- efficiency 효율성
- resource 자원

Model Answer

STEP 1 I agree that it is easier to come up with creative new ideas when working in a group than when working alone.
STEP 2 First of all, I think working in a group can improve work efficiency.
Another reason is that I believe that a group can share more ideas with one another.
STEP 3 For example, I'm a team player, and I usually focus a lot better when working in a team.
In my case, I had a team project two weeks ago, and we were able to come up with great ideas really quickly and get the job done.
STEP 4 Therefore, I agree with the statement that it is easier to come up with creative new ideas when working in a group than when working alone.

MINI TEST

🎧 C1 P5 Mini Test

TOEIC Speaking Question 11 of 11 Volume

Do you agree or disagree with the statement?
Traditional classroom learning is better than individual online learning.
Give specific reasons and examples to support your opinion.

PREPARATION TIME	RESPONSE TIME
00:00:45	00:00:60

HINT ANSWER STRUCTURE 답변 구조

STEP 1 I _____ that traditional classroom learning is better than individual online learning.

STEP 2 • First of all, _____.
• Also, _____.

STEP 3 • For example, _____.
• In my case, _____.

STEP 4 Therefore, I _____ with the statement.

Model Answer 모범 답안

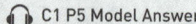 C1 P5 Model Answer

STEP 1 I disagree that traditional classroom learning is better than individual online learning.

STEP 2
- First of all, studying online can save time and money.
- Also, the Internet can be a good resource for education.

STEP 3
- For example, I was able to save a lot of time by studying online.
- In my case, I used my smartphone to access online classes, and I was able to take them whenever and wherever I wanted.

STEP 4 Therefore, I disagree with the statement that traditional classroom learning is better than individual online learning.

Translation 해석

문제

다음 문장에 동의합니까, 동의하지 않습니까?
교실에서 공부하는 전통적인 방식이 개개인이 온라인으로 학습하는 것보다 낫다.
구체적인 근거와 사례를 들어 의견을 뒷받침하십시오.

모범 답안

STEP 1 교실에서 공부하는 전통적인 방식을 유지하는 것이 혼자서 온라인으로 공부하는 것보다 낫다는 데 동의하지 않습니다.

STEP 2 우선, 온라인으로 공부하면 돈과 시간을 절약할 수 있습니다.
또한, 인터넷은 교육을 위한 좋은 자원이 될 수 있습니다.

STEP 3 예를 들어, 저는 온라인으로 공부함으로써 많은 시간을 절약했습니다.
저의 경우, 스마트폰으로 온라인 수업에 접속하여 언제 어디서든 편리하게 수업을 들을 수 있었습니다.

STEP 4 따라서, 저는 교실에서 공부하는 전통적인 방식을 유지하는 것이 혼자서 온라인으로 공부하는 것보다 낫다는 데 동의하지 않습니다.

REVIEW TEST 1

TOEIC Speaking — Question 1 of 11 — Volume

Are you planning your summer trip? Let the team at Travel Wise help you find the best deals on airline tickets, hotel reservations, and tours. For more than twenty years, our travel agency has been providing personalized service and convenience to travelers. Whether your travel is international or domestic, our team could make your trip a success.

PREPARATION TIME	RESPONSE TIME
00:00:45	00:00:45

TOEIC Speaking — Question 2 of 11 — Volume

Are you looking for exciting local activities happening this weekend? Well, we have good news for you. El Sobrante is holding its annual street fair this Saturday and Sunday. All weekend, there will be entertainment booths, food trucks, and vendor stalls along Vista Street. If you are in the area, you don't want to miss this delightful festival.

PREPARATION TIME	RESPONSE TIME
00:00:45	00:00:45

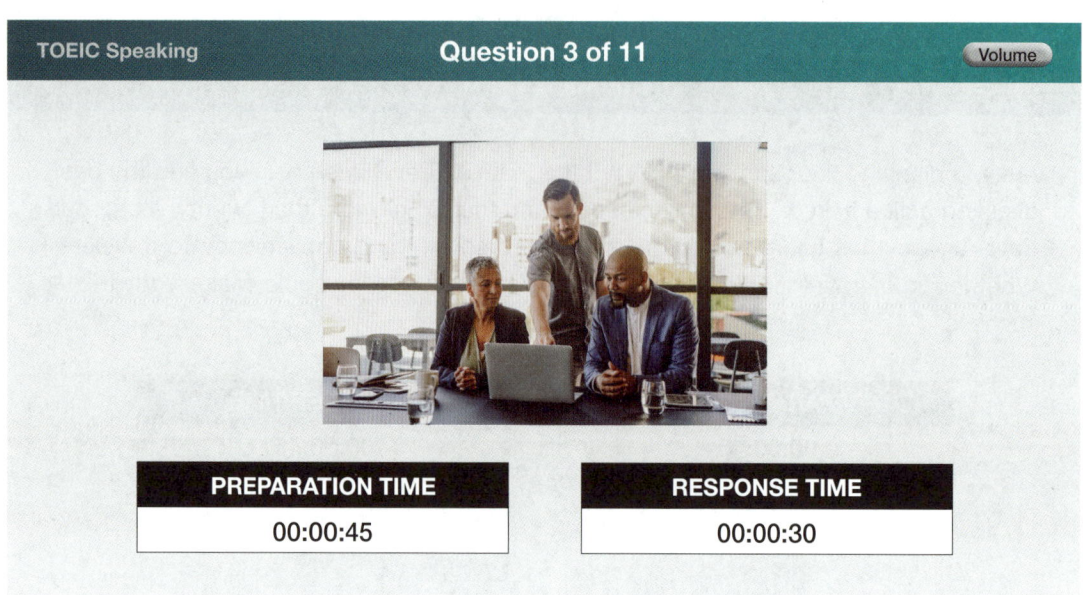

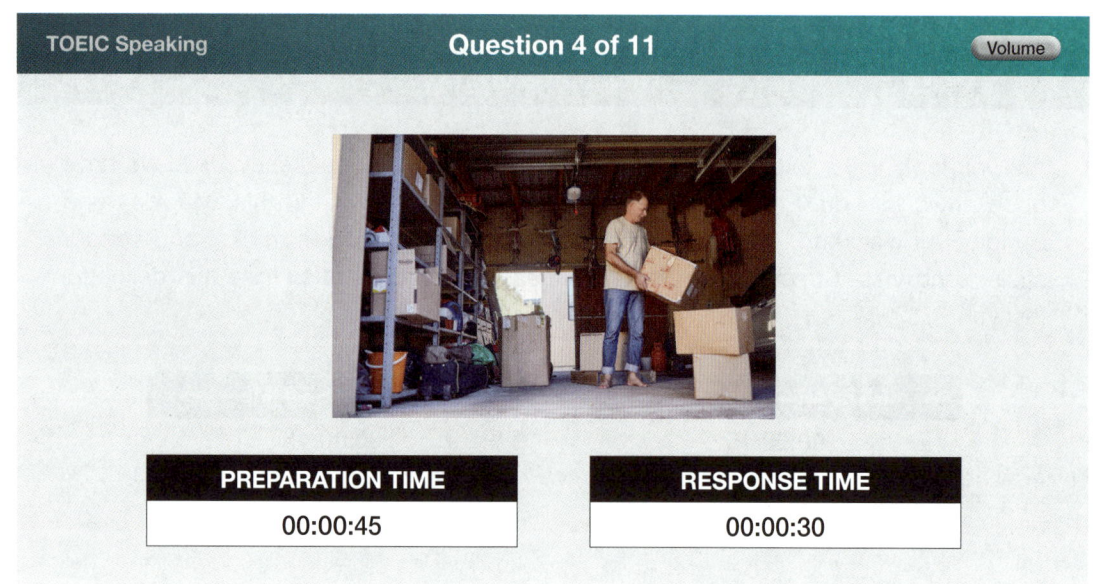

| TOEIC Speaking | Question 5 of 11 | Volume |

Imagine that someone wants to open a snack shop in your area. You have agreed to participate in a telephone interview about snacks.

What is your favorite snack, and how often do you eat it?

PREPARATION TIME	RESPONSE TIME
00:00:03	00:00:15

| TOEIC Speaking | Question 6 of 11 | Volume |

Imagine that someone wants to open a snack shop in your area. You have agreed to participate in a telephone interview about snacks.

Where do you usually have your snacks? Why?

PREPARATION TIME	RESPONSE TIME
00:00:03	00:00:15

| TOEIC Speaking | Question 7 of 11 | Volume |

Imagine that someone wants to open a snack shop in your area. You have agreed to participate in a telephone interview about snacks.

What would most influence your decision to purchase a certain snack?
- Taste
- Freshness
- Nutrition

PREPARATION TIME	RESPONSE TIME
00:00:03	00:00:30

TOEIC Speaking

Question 8-10 of 11

	Annual Conference for Landscape Designer's Association Eastville Conference Center Tuesday, Mar. 4 Cost (Members: $40 / Non-members: $60)	
Time	**Session**	**Presenter**
9:00 ~ 10:00 a.m.	Welcome speech & Breakfast	Chris Adams
10:00 ~ 11:00 a.m.	Lecture: Designing public spaces	Betsy King
11:00 a.m. ~ Noon	Workshop: New landscaping tools	Paul Mason
Noon ~ 1:00 p.m.	Lunch (buffet)	
1:00 ~ 2:00 p.m.	Demonstration: Computer drafting	Chris Adams
2:00 ~ 3:00 p.m.	Workshop: Identifying tree pests	William Gates
3:00 ~ 4:00 p.m.	Q & A: Residential landscaping	Timothy Steinberg

PREPARATION TIME
00:00:45

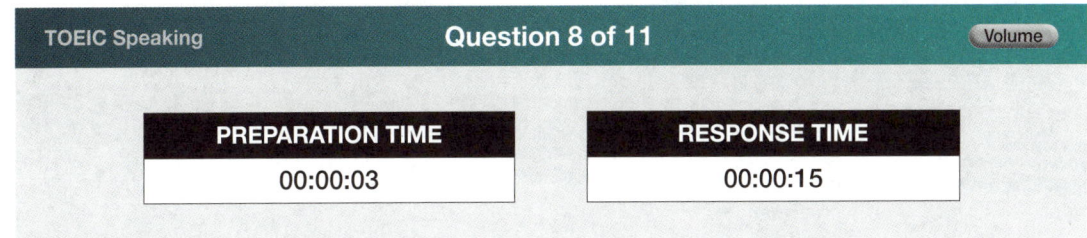

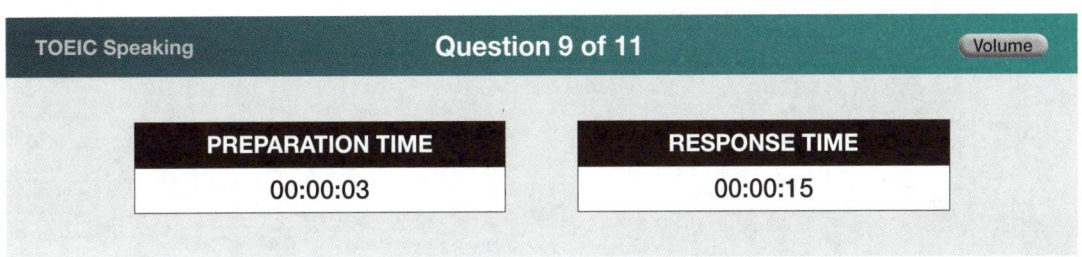

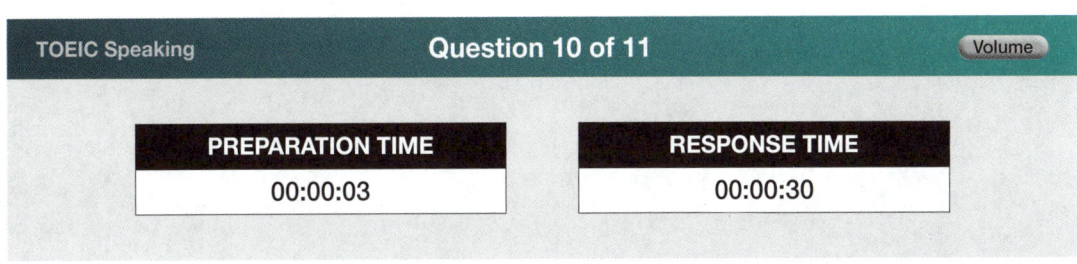

Do you agree or disagree with the following statement?
A successful employee must be able to work on multiple tasks at the same time.
Give reasons or examples to support your opinion.

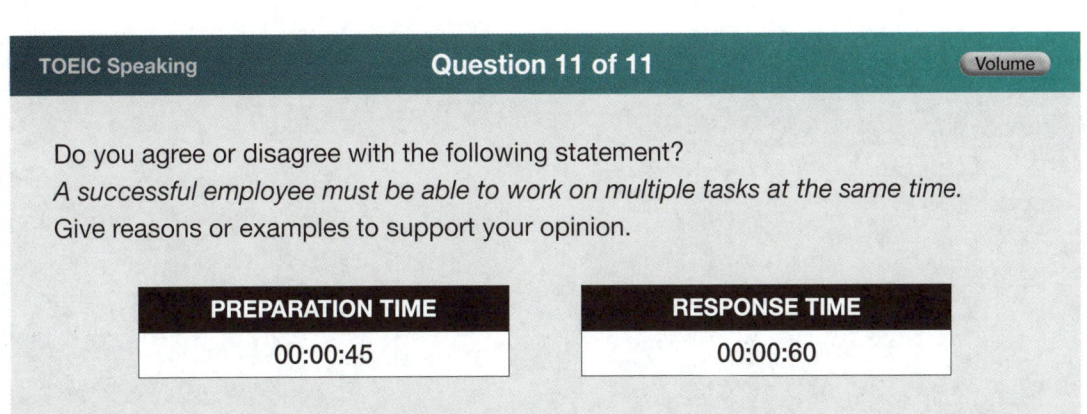

Chapter 2

PART 1
Read a text aloud

PART 2
Describe a picture

PART 3
Respond to questions

PART 4
Respond to questions using information provided

PART 5
Express an opinion

REVIEW TEST 2

PART 1 Read a text aloud

GROUNDWORK

📍 Master The Basics 이론 학습

Background Knowledge 배경 지식

Read the explanations and practice the "s" sound and linking sound that a lot of Koreans find difficult.
다음 설명을 읽고 한국인이 어려워하는 's' 소리와 연음을 익혀 보세요.

"S" sound	Be sure to pay attention to the "s", "es", and possessive " 's" at the end of a word and pronounce them. Oftentimes, these are left out when reading texts. **e.g.** part**s**, bark**s**, differenc**es**, today'**s**
Linking sound	Practice the part where the pronunciation changes as the two words are connected. This will help you speak naturally and fluently in English. **e.g.** re**d d**ress, nee**d t**o, a**n a**pple, today'**s s**ession

Practice 적용 연습

Read the given expressions aloud while paying attention to the "s" sound and linking sound.
's' 소리와 연음에 유의하여 주어진 표현을 소리 내어 읽어 보세요.

"S" sound
- product**s**, heart**s**, gat**es**, text**s**
- park**s**, tak**es**, mak**es**, cak**es**
- applianc**es**, influenc**es**, teleconferenc**es**
- company'**s**, restaurant'**s**, park'**s**, parents'

Linking sound
- fee**l l**ucky, quie**t t**own, ni**ce s**carf
- chee**se s**andwich, brea**the th**rough
- the**se a**re, Joe bough**t an a**pple
- nex**t f**ew, eve**n if y**ou, ha**ve a**, fro**m i**t

◉ Type Analysis: Notice/Guide 유형 분석: 공지/안내문

- Notice/Guide are texts that provide information about a notice or change to customers of a business, users of a transportation system, or employees of a company.
- It is one of the most frequently appearing text types in PART 1.
- It is important to read clearly and emphasize key words.

Useful Expressions 유용한 표현

These are the vocabulary and expressions commonly found in the notice/guide type texts of PART 1. Try to learn the meanings and pronunciations of each.
다음은 PART 1 지문 유형 중 공지/안내문에 자주 쓰이는 어휘 및 표현들입니다. 각각의 뜻을 익혀 보세요.

- pay attention (to) (~에) 주목하다
- join 함께하다, 합류하다
- especially 특별히
- make sure ~을 확실히 하다
- encourage 장려하다
- be sure to 반드시 ~하다
- provided 제공된
- restriction 제한
- requested 요청받은
- mandatory 필수적인
- keep in mind 명심하다
- announce 발표하다
- consist of ~으로 구성되다
- facility 시설
- regardless of ~에 상관없이
- participate 참여하다

Practice 적용 연습

Read the given passage with a calm and assertive tone of voice while paying attention to the intonation marks.
억양 기호에 주의하며 주어진 지문을 차분하고 단호한 어조로 읽어 보세요.

> Welcome to today's session on "Correct Leadership" in the workplace. For the next few days, you'll gain helpful tips and strategies on motivating employees, ↗ handling changes at work, ↗ and connecting with your colleagues. ↘ Even if you already have a leadership position at your job, you can still benefit from it. So, let's get started without further ado. ↘

MINI TEST

🎧 C2 P1 Mini Test, 🎧 C2 P1 Model Answer

TOEIC Speaking Question 1 of 11 Volume

Welcome everyone to the Sweets Candy Factory! We are excited to show you around the factory, which is celebrating its sixtieth anniversary. You will watch a video about our history, production line, and most popular candies. After the video, you will be able to purchase your favorites at our gift shop. We have limited time. So, let's get started!

PREPARATION TIME	RESPONSE TIME
00:00:45	00:00:45

Translation 해석

Sweets Candy Factory에 오신 것을 환영합니다! 창립 60주년을 맞이해 여러분께 저희 공장을 보여 드리게 되어 기쁩니다. 여러분께서는 공장의 역사, 생산 라인, 그리고 가장 인기 있는 제품과 관련된 영상을 시청하시게 될 겁니다. 영상이 끝나면, 여러분에서 가장 좋아하시는 제품들을 기념품 가게에서 구매하실 수 있습니다. 시간이 얼마 없습니다. 그러니, 바로 시작하죠!

TOEIC Speaking | Question 2 of 11 |

Welcome to Marine Cinema of Emeryville City. Please keep in mind that all mobile phones should be put in silent mode or turned off. Note that the emergency exits are on each side of the building. Also, don't forget to take all your belongings with you on your way out. Now, sit back, relax, and enjoy the movie.

PREPARATION TIME	RESPONSE TIME
00:00:45	00:00:45

Translation 해석

Emeryville City의 Marine Cinema에 오신 것을 환영합니다. 모든 휴대 전화는 무음으로 설정하거나 전원을 꺼야 하신다는 점을 유의해 주세요. 비상구는 건물 양쪽에 있습니다. 또한, 나가시는 길에 가지고 오신 모든 소지품을 잘 챙기셨는지 확인해 주세요. 이제, 편히 앉아 긴장을 푸시고, 영화를 즐겨 주시길 바랍니다.

PART 2 | Describe a picture

GROUNDWORK

📍 Type Analysis: Shop/Restaurant 유형 분석: 가게/식당

Useful Expression 유용한 표현

These are the vocabulary and expressions that can be used when describing a picture taken in a shop/restaurant in PART 2. Try to learn the meanings and pronunciations of each.
다음은 PART 2 사진 유형 중 가게/식당에서 찍힌 사진을 묘사할 때 유용하게 쓸 수 있는 어휘 및 표현들입니다. 각각의 뜻을 익혀 보세요.

- employee 직원
- server (성별 구분 없이) 웨이터
- apron 앞치마
- staff uniform 직원 근무복
- order 주문하다
- take orders 주문을 받다
- unoccupied (의자, 테이블 등이) 비어 있는
- set up 준비하다
- have a meal 식사하다
- place 놓다
- be displayed 진열되어 있다
- well-organized 잘 정리된
- purchase 구매하다
- try on 입어 보다
- pay for ~에 대한 금액을 지불하다
- pay by ~로 지불하다

Sample Practice 예제 연습

Ideation

Look at the picture and think about what you want to focus on when describing it.
다음 사진을 보고, 무엇을 묘사할 것인지 생각해 보세요.

- Where do you think this picture was taken?
- How many people do you see in this picture?
- What do you think the man on the right and the woman in the middle are doing?
- In the back, there is a couple. How old do they look?
- What else do you see in the store?
- What do you feel when you look at the picture?

Answer Structure

Now, follow the steps below to organize your response systematically.
이제, 아래 단계에 따라 답변을 체계적으로 구성해 보세요.

STEP 1 — Place & Number of people

Begin by stating the location where the picture might have been taken. If possible, also mention the number of people in the picture.

Pattern 1
This picture was taken in a(n) _____.
- grocery store   • supermarket

Pattern 2
I see _____ people in this picture.
- four   • several

STEP 2 — Main person or thing

Describe the main person or thing in the picture.

Pattern
The first thing I'm noticing is a(n) _____.
- employee helping a customer   • woman paying for the items

STEP 3 — Surroundings

Say a few things about the rest of the picture by using location descriptions.

Pattern 1
Behind them, _____.
- I see a couple waiting in line

Pattern 2
In the foreground of the picture, _____.
- I see a shopping basket filled with groceries

Pattern 3
Also, _____.
- many items are displayed at the store

STEP 4 — Opinions or feelings about the picture

Conclude by expressing your thoughts or feelings about the picture.

Pattern 1
It seems like _____.
- a typical scene from a supermarket

Pattern 2
I like/don't like this picture because _____.
- it reminds me of my part-time job

MINI TEST

C2 P2 Mini Test

HINT 1 Answer Structure 답변 구조

This picture was taken at a restaurant. I can see several people in this picture.

❶ The first thing I notice is _____.

❷ Next to the _____, _____.

❸ In front of _____, _____.

❹ In the background, _____.

I like this picture because it reminds me of my favorite restaurant.

HINT 2 Useful Expression 유용한 표현

- restaurant
  식당
- apron
  앞치마
- ask about the menu
  메뉴에 대해 묻다
- wine glass
  와인 잔
- be placed on
  ~에 놓여 있다
- a group of people
  단체
- facial hair
  수염
- have a good time
  좋은 시간을 보내다
- good vibe
  좋은 분위기

TOEIC Speaking   Question 4 of 11

PREPARATION TIME	RESPONSE TIME
00:00:45	00:00:30

HINT 1 Answer Structure 답변 구조

I think this picture was taken at an outdoor café.

❶ The first thing I notice is _____.

❷ On the right, _____.

❸ In the background, _____.

I like this picture because the people in it seem happy and carefree.

HINT 2 Useful Expression 유용한 표현

- outdoor café
  야외 카페
- spring
  봄
- smiling
  미소 짓는
- blurry
  흐릿한
- ponytail
  하나로 묶은 머리
- unoccupied chair
  비어 있는 의자
- parasol
  파라솔
- late afternoon
  늦은 오후
- salt shaker
  식탁에 놓는 소금통
- rectangular table
  네모난 탁자
- carefree
  근심이 없는, 속편한

Chapter 2   PART 2 Describe a picture   57

Model Answer 모범 답안

🎧 C2 P2 Model Answer

3. This picture was taken at a restaurant. I can see several people in this picture.

   ❶ **The first thing I notice is** a server taking an order. He is wearing a black apron.

   ❷ **Next to the** server, a man wearing a blue jacket is sitting at a table. I think he is asking about the menu.

   ❸ **In front of** him, a glass of wine and a bottle are placed on the table.

   ❹ **In the background,** it looks like a group of women are enjoying their meals.

   I like this picture because it reminds me of my favorite restaurant.

4. I think this picture was taken at an outdoor café.

   ❶ **The first thing I notice is** three women sitting at a table, enjoying their time.

   ❷ **On the right,** I can see a man sitting by himself.

   ❸ **In the background,** it is quite blurry, but it looks like there are many people sitting under red parasols.

   I like this picture because the people in it seem happy and carefree.

Translation 해석

3. 이 사진은 식당에서 찍힌 사진입니다. 이 사진에서 여러 사람을 볼 수 있습니다.
   ❶ **가장 먼저 눈에 띄는 것은** 주문을 받는 웨이터입니다. 그는 검정색 앞치마를 걸치고 있습니다.
   ❷ 웨이터의 **옆에는** 파란색 재킷을 입은 남자가 앉아 있습니다. 그는 메뉴에 대해 묻는 것 같습니다.
   ❸ 그의 **앞에는** 와인 한 잔과 병이 탁자 위에 놓여 있습니다.
   ❹ **배경에는** 단체로 온 여성 손님들이 식사를 즐기고 있는 것처럼 보입니다.
   이 사진이 마음에 드는 이유는 제가 가장 좋아하는 식당을 생각나게 하기 때문입니다.

4. 이 사진은 야외 카페에서 찍힌 것 같습니다.
   ❶ **가장 먼저 눈에 띄는 것은** 탁자에 앉아 그들의 시간을 즐기고 있는 세 명의 여자들입니다.
   ❷ **오른쪽에는** 혼자 앉아 있는 남자가 보입니다.
   ❸ **배경에는**, 흐릿하기는 하지만 빨간색 파라솔 아래 많은 사람들이 앉아 있는 것처럼 보입니다.
   사진 속 사람들이 행복하고 근심 없어 보여 이 사진이 좋습니다.

PART 3 Respond to questions

GROUNDWORK

📍 Master The Basics 이론 학습

Background Knowledge 배경 지식

We will now take a look at some idea patterns to quickly come up with the key answer and further explanation for questions in PART 3. It is important to use these patterns on the test because the preparation time for questions 5, 6, 7 is only 3 seconds.

이제 PART 3에서 출제되는 질문에 빠르게 답하기 위해 사용할 수 있는 몇 가지 소재 패턴을 학습할 것입니다. 5번부터 7번까지는 답변 준비 시간이 단 3초이기 때문에, 이 패턴들을 익혀 두었다가 활용하는 것이 중요합니다.

Money

You can talk about how certain things affect you financially.

e.g. **Question:** How often do you eat out?
Answer: I eat out only once a week. That's because it costs a lot of money to eat out.

Time

You can talk about how certain things affect your time.

e.g. **Question:** How often do you eat out?
Answer: I eat out only once a week. That's because I don't have a lot of time to eat out.

Convenience & Comfort

You can talk about whether certain things are convenient or comfortable.

e.g. **Question:** How often do you eat out?
Answer: I eat out three times a week. That's because it is very convenient for me not to have to cook.

Quality

You can talk about whether the quality of certain things are good or bad.

e.g. **Question:** How often do you eat out?
Answer: I eat out three times a week. That's because the taste is of much better quality than when I cook for myself.

Practice 적용 연습

Based on what you have learned, practice answering the following questions.
학습한 내용을 바탕으로, 다음 질문에 답변해 보세요.

Question

1. **Question:** Where do you usually go shopping?
   Answer: I usually go shopping _____. That's because _____.

2. **Question:** Who do you usually go shopping with?
   Answer: I usually go shopping (with) _____. That's because _____.

3. **Question:** What do you think are some advantages of shopping online?
   Answer:
   - **Topic sentence** I think there are some _____.
   - **Time killer** _____.
   - **Reason 1** First of all, _____.
   - **Reason 2** Also, _____.
   - **Wrap up** These are some advantages of _____.

Model Answer

1. at the department store, I can trust the product quality
2. alone, it's time-saving if I go alone
3.
   - **Topic sentence** advantages of shopping online
   - **Time killer** I have a few reasons why
   - **Reason 1** shopping online saves money and time
   - **Reason 2** I think it is the most convenient way to shop
   - **Wrap up** shopping online

MINI TEST

TOEIC Speaking   Question 5 of 11

Imagine that a US marketing firm is doing research in your country. You have agreed to participate in a telephone interview about traveling.

How often do you travel? And do you usually travel alone?

PREPARATION TIME	RESPONSE TIME
00:00:03	00:00:15

TOEIC Speaking   Question 6 of 11

Imagine that a US marketing firm is doing research in your country. You have agreed to participate in a telephone interview about traveling.

When you travel, do you travel with a lot of baggage? Why or why not?

PREPARATION TIME	RESPONSE TIME
00:00:03	00:00:15

TOEIC Speaking   Question 7 of 11

Imagine that a US marketing firm is doing research in your country. You have agreed to participate in a telephone interview about traveling.

Do you prefer to travel by train or by airplane?

PREPARATION TIME	RESPONSE TIME
00:00:03	00:00:30

Model Answer 모범 답안

🎧 C2 P3 Model Answer

5. I normally travel twice a year. I usually travel alone because I feel more comfortable.

6. When I travel, I don't travel with a lot of baggage. That's because it is very inconvenient and drains my energy.

7.
   - **Topic sentence**: I prefer to travel by plane.
   - **Time killer**: I have a few reasons why.
   - **Reason 1**: First of all, traveling by plane saves me time. I can get to the destination and back much faster.
   - **Reason 2**: Also, It's more cost-effective because my dad works for an airline company, and I get a discount.
   - **Wrap up**: So, I prefer to travel by plane.

Translation 해석

상황 설정

미국의 한 마케팅 회사가 여러분의 국가에서 조사를 진행하고 있다고 가정해 봅시다. 여러분은 여행에 대한 유선 설문 조사에 응하기로 했습니다.

5번 질문, 모범 답안

Q: 당신은 얼마나 자주 여행을 가시나요? 그리고 보통 혼자 여행 하시나요?
A: 저는 보통 1년에 두 번 여행을 갑니다. 주로 혼자 여행을 가는데, 그것이 더 편하기 때문입니다.

6번 질문, 모범 답안

Q: 여행할 때 짐을 많이 가지고 다니나요? 왜 그런가요?
A: 저는 여행할 때 짐을 많이 가지고 다니지 않습니다. 아주 불편하고 에너지를 많이 소모하게 되기 때문입니다.

7번 질문, 모범 답안

Q: 기차와 비행기 중 어떤 수단으로 여행하는 것을 선호합니까?
A:
   - **Topic sentence**: 저는 비행기로 여행하는 것을 선호합니다.
   - **Time killer**: 몇 가지 이유가 있습니다.
   - **Reason 1**: 우선, 비행기로 여행하면 시간이 절약됩니다. 목적지까지 훨씬 더 빠르게 왕복할 수 있습니다.
   - **Reason 2**: 또한, 아버지가 항공사에 재직 중이셔서 할인을 받을 수 있기 때문에 비용 절약도 할 수 있습니다.
   - **Wrap Up**: 그래서, 저는 비행기로 여행하는 것을 선호합니다.

PART 4 Respond to questions using information provided

GROUNDWORK

📍 Master The Basics 이론 학습

Background Knowledge 배경 지식

In PART 4, there is a high probability of questions asking about schedules. Learn the following basics to familiarize yourself with how to express dates and times in English using the appropriate prepositions.

PART4에서는 높은 확률로 일정을 묻는 문제가 출제됩니다. 따라서, 일자와 시간을 영어로 어떻게 표현하는지 알아둘 필요가 있습니다. 이어지는 내용을 학습하여 각 경우에 어떤 전치사를 사용하면 되는지 익혀 두세요.

---

on

When talking about the exact dates, such as months, dates, and days of the week, the preposition "on" is used.

e.g.
- The conference will be held on August 28.
- The interview will be held on Wednesday.

in

The preposition "in" can be used for both time and place. When talking about year or month, you can use the preposition "in." Also, when referring to a specific location where an event is taking place, you can use "in" to describe it.

e.g.
- The workshop will be held in January.
- The demonstration will be held in Classroom A.

at

When talking about the exact time an event starts, you can use "at." Moreover, when referring to a location where an event is taking place, you can use "at" as well.

e.g.
- The keynote speech will be held at the Joy Conference Center.
- The presentation will be given at 11:00 a.m.

from A to B

"From A to B" is an expression that can be used to talk about the starting and ending points of an event. You can use "from" followed by the starting point and "to" followed by the ending point.

e.g.
- The manager's meeting will be held from 9:00 a.m. to 10:30 a.m.
- The film festival will be held from Thursday to Sunday.

for & per

When talking about the expenses or costs, you can use the prepositions "for" or "per." After "for," you can mention the specific target to which the cost applies, and after "per," you can mention a unit such as "per person" or "per group."

e.g.
- The price is fifteen dollars for adults and three dollars for children.
- The cost is 25 dollars per person.

Practice 적용 연습

Based on what you have learned, answer the following questions.
학습한 내용을 바탕으로, 다음 질문에 답변해 보세요.

Question

West Coast Car Exhibition
Saturday, Apr. 10 ~ Sunday, Apr. 11
Ilsan Convention Center

Saturday	
10:00 a.m.	New features in current vehicles (Demonstration)
11:00 a.m.	Options in electric vehicles for the environment (Presentation)
2:00 p.m.	Brand new car models (Car parade)
3:00 p.m.	Winning safety features (Award Ceremony)
Sunday	
11:00 a.m.	Sports car models from the 70's and 80's (Presentation)
1:00 p.m.	Environmentally friendly solar-powered vehicles (Demonstration)

1. What are the dates of the event, and where will it be held?
2. I heard that the award ceremony has been canceled this year. Is that right?
3. I'm particularly interested in sessions related to the environment. Can you give me all the details of the events that deal with the environment?

Model Answer

1. The exhibition will be held on Saturday, April 10th and on Sunday, April 11th at the Ilsan Convention Center.

2. Actually, you have the wrong information. The award ceremony will be held on Saturday at 3 p.m.

3. Sure. There are two sessions related to the environment. First, on Saturday at 11 a.m., a presentation on environmental options in electric vehicles will be held. Also, a demonstration on environmentally friendly solar-powered vehicles will be held on Sunday at 1 p.m.

MINI TEST

🎧 C2 P4 Mini Test

TOEIC Speaking — Question 8-10 of 11

	Annual Educational Technology Conference *Aug. 28, Valley Convention Center* Registration fee : $60
8:00 a.m.~ 9:00 a.m.	Registration and Breakfast Pack
9:00 a.m. ~ 10:00 a.m.	Keynote Speech: Inspirational Learning (Robert Dickerson)
10:00 a.m. ~ Noon	Workshop: Multimedia for Science Education (Kendall Jackson)
Noon ~ 1:30 p.m.	Lunch (Center Cafeteria)
1:30 p.m. ~ 3:30 p.m.	Training: Art Projects Using Tablet PCs (Mike Kim)
3:30 p.m. ~ 4:30 p.m.	Demonstration: Online Science Games (Dru Hill)

PREPARATION TIME
00:00:45

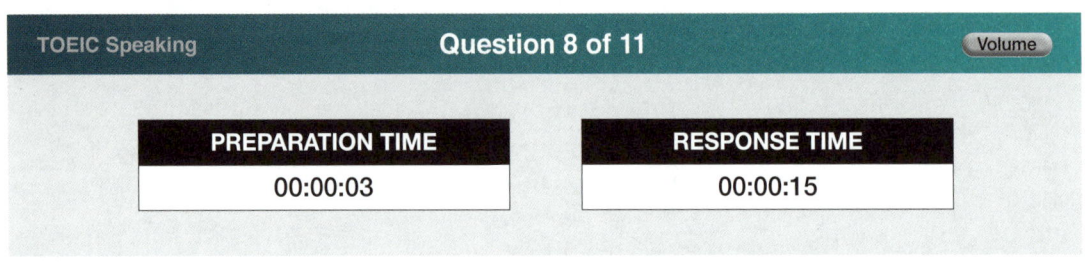

HINT Useful Expression 유용한 표현

- date 일자
- location 장소
- be held 개최되다
- on (구체적인 날짜)에
- at (장소)에서

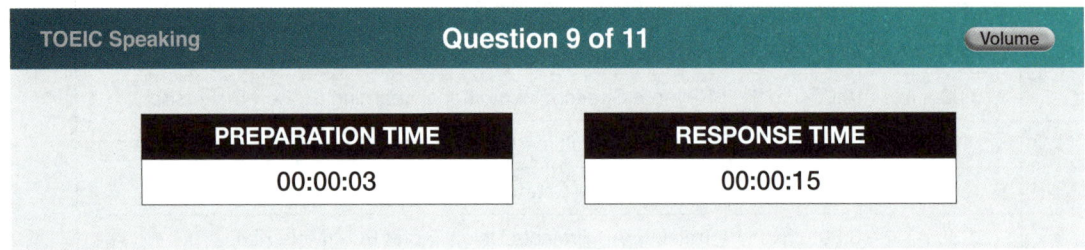

HINT Useful Expression 유용한 표현

- cost 비용이 들다
- I am afraid that … 유감이지만 …입니다
- attend 참석하다
- registration 등록
- be the same 같다
- fee 비용

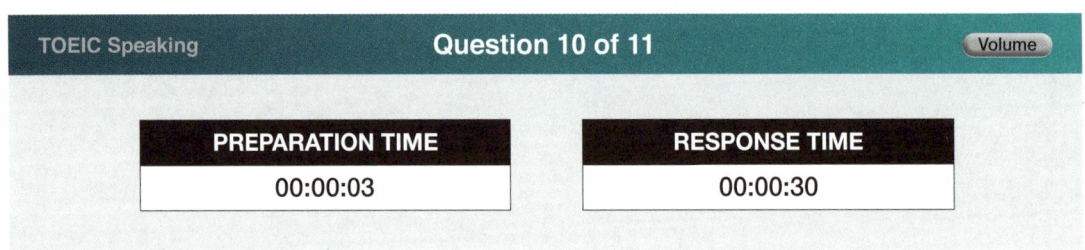

HINT Useful Expression 유용한 표현

- look forward to ~을 고대하다
- specifically 특별히, 구체적으로
- session 강의, 세션
- about ~에 관련해
- deal with ~을 다루다
- from A to B A부터 B까지

Model Answer 모범 답안

🎧 C2 P4 Model Answer

	Annual Educational Technology Conference ❽ Aug. 28, Valley Convention Center Registration fee : ❾ $60
8:00 a.m. ~ 9:00 a.m.	Registration and Breakfast Pack
9:00 a.m. ~ 10:00 a.m.	Keynote Speech: Inspirational Learning (Robert Dickerson)
❿ 10:00 a.m. ~ Noon	Workshop: Multimedia for Science Education (Kendall Jackson)
Noon ~ 1:30 p.m.	Lunch (Center Cafeteria)
1:30 p.m. ~ 3:30 p.m.	Training: Art Projects Using Tablet PCs (Mike Kim)
❿ 3:30 p.m. ~ 4:30 p.m.	Demonstration: Online Science Games (Dru Hill)

Narration: Hello, I'm a school teacher, and I'm very interested in the upcoming conference in August. I have a few questions about it that I am hoping you can answer.

8. Question: Can you tell me the date and location of the conference?
   Answer: The conference will be held on August 28th at the Valley Convention Center.

9. Question: It cost 50 dollars to attend the conference last year. It's the same this year, right?
   Answer: Actually, you have the wrong information. The registration fee is 60 dollars this year.

10. Question: I'm mostly looking forward to sessions about science. Could you give me the details about the sessions that deal specifically with science?
   Answer: Sure. There are two sessions about science. First, a workshop on Multimedia for Science Education will be held from 10 a.m. to noon. It will be led by Kendall Jackson. Second, a demonstration on Online Science Games will be held from 3:30 p.m. to 4:30 p.m. It will be led by Dru Hill.

Translation 해석

나레이션
안녕하세요. 저는 교사이고, 다가오는 8월에 있을 학회에 매우 관심이 있습니다. 관련해서 몇 가지 문의를 드리고 싶어요.

8번 질문, 모범 답안
Q: 회의 날짜와 장소를 알려 주시겠습니까?
A: 학회는 8월 28일 Valley Convention Center에서 개최됩니다.

9번 질문, 모범 답안
Q: 작년 학회에 참석하는 데 50달러가 들었습니다. 올해도 마찬가지인가요?
A: 사실, 잘못 알고 계십니다. 올해 등록 비용은 60달러입니다.

10번 질문, 모범 답안
Q: 저는 주로 과학 관련 세션을 기대하고 있습니다. 과학을 구체적으로 다루는 세션에 대해 자세히 알려주실 수 있습니까?
A: 물론이죠. 과학 관련 세션은 두 가지가 있습니다. 먼저 오전 10시부터 정오까지 '다중 매체로 과학 가르치기' 워크숍이 진행됩니다. 이는 Kendall Jackson에 의해 진행될 예정입니다. 두 번째는 오후 3시 30분부터 4시 30분까지 진행되는 '온라인 과학 게임'의 시연회입니다. Dru Hill이 해당 세션을 진행할 것입니다.

PART 5 Express an opinion

GROUNDWORK

◉ Type Analysis: Advantage/Disadvantage 유형 분석: 장/단점 질문

Background Knowledge 배경 지식

In this unit, we will practice how to respond to questions asking about "advantages/disadvantages." Most of the questions in PART 5 are related to professions, work, education, and lifestyle. Therefore, it is essential to prepare various ideas related to these topics.

이번 단원에서는 '장/단점'을 묻는 질문 유형에 답변하는 방법을 연습할 것입니다. PART 5에서 출제되는 대부분의 질문은 직업, 업무, 교육, 그리고 생활 방식과 관련되어 있으니 이와 관련하여 다양한 아이디어를 준비해 놓을 필요가 있습니다.

Question Example

What are the advantages of having a flexible work schedule?
Give specific reasons and examples to support your answer.

Answer Structure

Keep the following order in mind to respond to the question in a more organized manner.
다음 순서에 유념하여 답변을 논리적으로 구성해 보세요.

STEP 1 | Paraphrase the question

Refer to the given sentence pattern below and start off your argument by paraphrasing the question.

| Expression to use | There are several(many) _____ . |

e.g. **There are many several(many)** advantages/disadvantages to having a flexible work schedule.

STEP 2 — Explain your reasons

Explain reasons for your argument using the following expressions.

Expression to use
- First of all, _____.
- In addition to that, _____.
- Last but not least, _____.

e.g. **First of all,** it helps improve your work and life balance.
Last but not least, you can avoid rush hour traffic, saving time and reducing commuting-related stress.

e.g. **First of all,** it is challenging to collaborate with my colleagues because everyone has different work schedules.
In addition to that, I sometimes find that I get easily distracted due to the thought that I can get my work done at a later time.

STEP 3 — Support your reasons using examples

Use your own experience as an example to support your claims. It doesn't affect the score if the examples are not true.

Expression to use
- For instance, _____.
- From my experience, _____.
- I heard that _____.

e.g. **For instance,** I had a flexible work schedule at my previous job.
From my experience, having a flexible work schedule allows you to achieve work-life balance, resulting in improving your productivity.

e.g. **I heard that** many of my colleagues also face the same challenge.

STEP 4 — Conclude

Finish your response by summarizing the argument.

Expression to use
- In conclusion, _____.
- Therefore, _____.

e.g. **In conclusion,** I think these are the advantages of having a flexible work schedule.
e.g. **Therefore,** I think there are some disadvantages to having a flexible work schedule.

Practice 적용 연습

Based on what you have learned, answer the following questions.
학습한 내용을 바탕으로, 다음 질문에 답변해 보세요.

Question

What are the advantages of starting a business with a friend?
Give specific reasons and examples to support your answer.

HINT 1 Answer Structure 답변 구조

STEP 1 Paraphrase the question
  I think there are many _____.

STEP 2 Explain your reasons
  - First of all, _____.
  - Also, _____.
  - Last but not least, _____.

STEP 3 Support your reasons using examples
  - For instance, _____.
  - From my experience, _____.

STEP 4 Conclude
  Therefore, _____.

HINT 2 Useful Expression 유용한 표현

- positive work relationships 긍정적인 업무 관계
- honest opinion 솔직한 의견
- trust 믿음
- share the same vision 같은 비전을 갖다
- strengths and weaknesses 강점과 약점
- better understanding 더 나은 이해
- less strict about ~에 덜 엄격한
- emotional support 정서적 지원
- job satisfaction 직업 만족도
- motivation 동기 부여

Model Answer

STEP 1 I think there are many advantages to starting a business with a friend.
STEP 2 First of all, I think the work will be more enjoyable.
Also, it is possible to work in a comfortable environment based on trust.
Last but not least, friends can communicate with better understanding of each other.
STEP 3 For instance, two of my close friends started a business together last year, and they seem to be having so much fun working together while having success.
STEP 4 Therefore, I think there are some advantages of starting a business with a friend.

MINI TEST

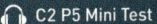

🎧 C2 P5 Mini Test

TOEIC Speaking Question 11 of 11 Volume

What are the advantages of taking a job in a foreign country?
Give specific reasons and examples to support your opinion.

PREPARATION TIME	RESPONSE TIME
00:00:45	00:00:60

HINT ANSWER STRUCTURE

- **STEP 1** I think there are many _____.
- **STEP 2** • First of all, _____.
  • Another reason is that _____.
- **STEP 3** • For instance, _____.
  • From my experience, _____.
- **STEP 4** Therefore, I think these are some _____.

Model Answer 모범 답안

🎧 C2 P5 Model Answer

STEP 1 I think there are many advantages to taking a job in a foreign country.
STEP 2 • First of all, I think it's a great opportunity to experience a different culture and meet new people.
• Another reason is that you can learn a new language naturally by communicating with foreigners.
STEP 3 For instance, I had a chance to work in Australia for a year, and I've made so many good friends. At the same time, my English has gotten so much better.
STEP 4 Therefore, I think these are some advantages of taking a job in a foreign country.

Translation 해석

문제
해외 취업의 장점이 무엇이라고 생각하십니까?
구체적인 근거와 사례를 들어 의견을 뒷받침하십시오.

모범 답안
STEP 1 저는 해외 취업의 장점이 **많다고 생각합니다**.
STEP 2 • **우선**, 다른 문화를 경험하고 새로운 사람들을 만날 수 있는 좋은 기회라고 생각합니다.
• **또 다른 이유는**, 외국인과의 의사소통을 통해 자연스럽게 새로운 언어를 배울 수 있다는 것입니다.
STEP 3 **예를 들어**, 저는 호주에서 1년 동안 일할 기회가 있었는데 그때 좋은 친구들을 많이 사귀었습니다. 그와 동시에 영어 실력도 많이 늘었습니다.
STEP 4 **따라서**, 이러한 것들이 외국에서 취업하는 것의 장점이라고 생각합니다.

REVIEW TEST 2

TOEIC Speaking Question 1 of 11   Volume

Welcome to the National Art Museum! On today's tour, we'll be looking at some of the most well-known paintings, photographs, and sculptures in our collection. Because backpacks and briefcases are not allowed in the exhibit area, please leave them here at the front desk. When everyone's ready, we'll begin with the sculptures by the stairs.

PREPARATION TIME	RESPONSE TIME
00:00:45	00:00:45

TOEIC Speaking Question 2 of 11   Volume

Welcome to the Miramar Swimming Pool. To make sure everyone has an enjoyable time, please follow these instructions. First, no drinks, snacks, or any other food items are allowed. Also, no street shoes are permitted near the swimming pool area. Please enjoy your time at the Miramar Swimming Pool!

PREPARATION TIME	RESPONSE TIME
00:00:45	00:00:45

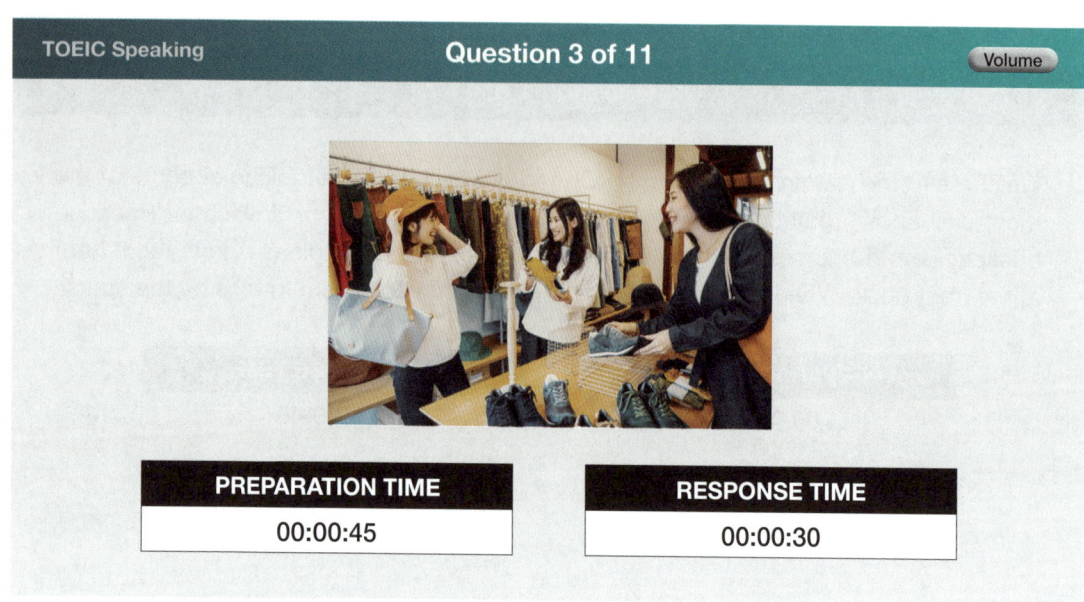

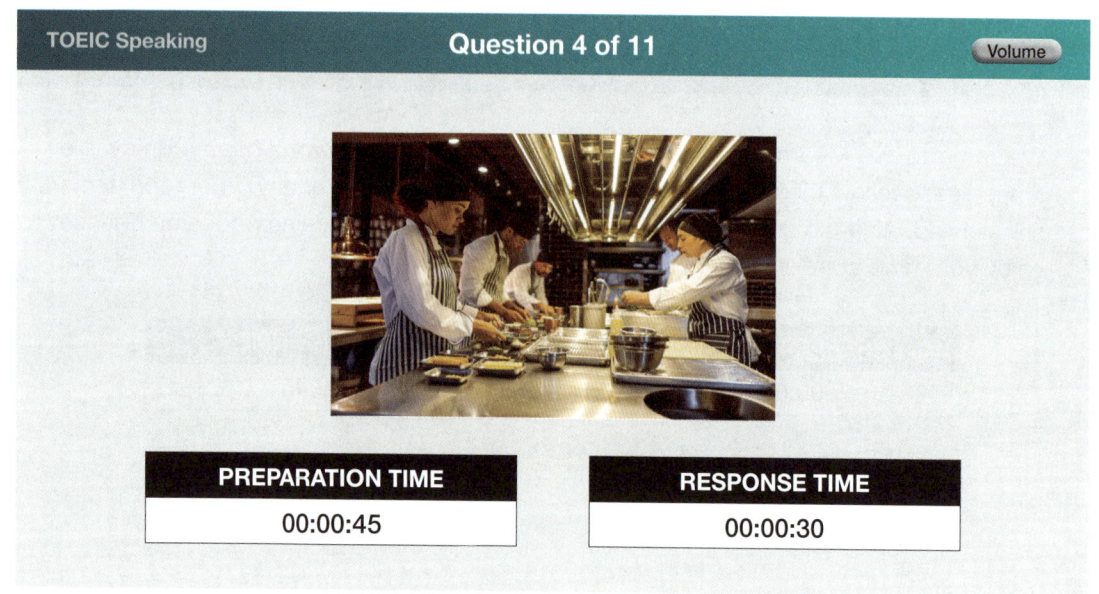

TOEIC Speaking Question 5 of 11

Imagine that a US marketing firm is doing research in your area. You have agreed to participate in a telephone interview about using email.

When was the last time you used your email, and how many email accounts do you have?

PREPARATION TIME	RESPONSE TIME
00:00:03	00:00:15

TOEIC Speaking Question 6 of 11

Imagine that a US marketing firm is doing research in your area. You have agreed to participate in a telephone interview about using email.

How much time do you spend on checking your email each day?

PREPARATION TIME	RESPONSE TIME
00:00:03	00:00:15

TOEIC Speaking Question 7 of 11 Volume

Imagine that a US marketing firm is doing research in your area. You have agreed to participate in a telephone interview about using email.

Do you think email exchanges are better than in-person meetings? Why or why not?

PREPARATION TIME	RESPONSE TIME
00:00:03	00:00:30

TOEIC Speaking Question 8-10 of 11

| \multicolumn{3}{c}{**Realcomm. Employee Retreat**} |
| Cross Creek Resort, July 12 |

Time	Schedule	Speaker
9:30 a.m. ~ 10:30 a.m.	Opening Remarks	George Brett, Manager
10:30 a.m. ~ Noon	Training: Managing Work Hours	Aaron Wood, Senior manager
Noon ~ 1:30 p.m.	Lunch (Outdoor Barbecue)	
1:30 p.m. ~ 3:00 p.m.	Recreational Event: Dodgeball	
3:00 p.m. ~ 4:00 p.m.	Break	
4:00 p.m. ~ 5:00 p.m.	Training: Effective Communication	William Gates, Manager
5:00 p.m. ~ 7:30 p.m.	Awards Ceremony & Buffet Dinner	Kenji Yamata, President

PREPARATION TIME
00:00:45

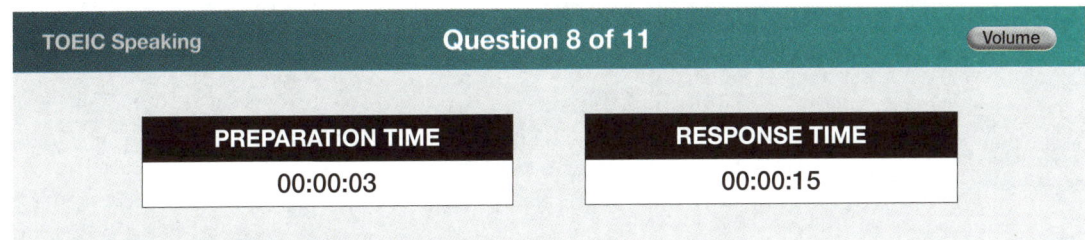

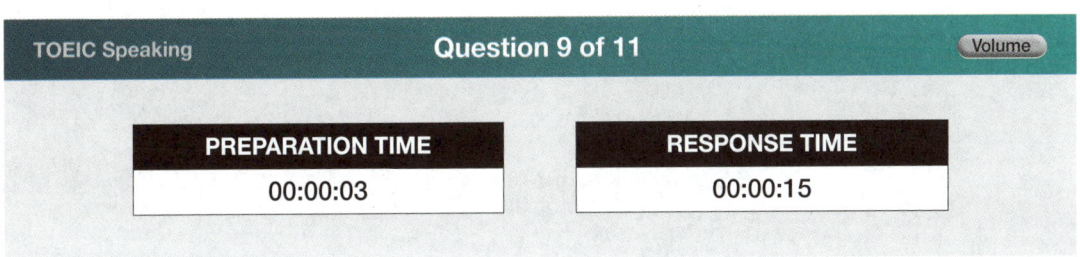

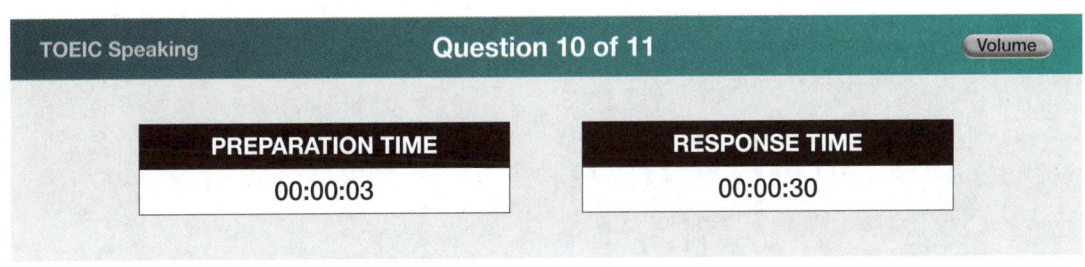

What are the advantages of living in a big city compared to living in a small city? Give reasons or examples to support your opinion.

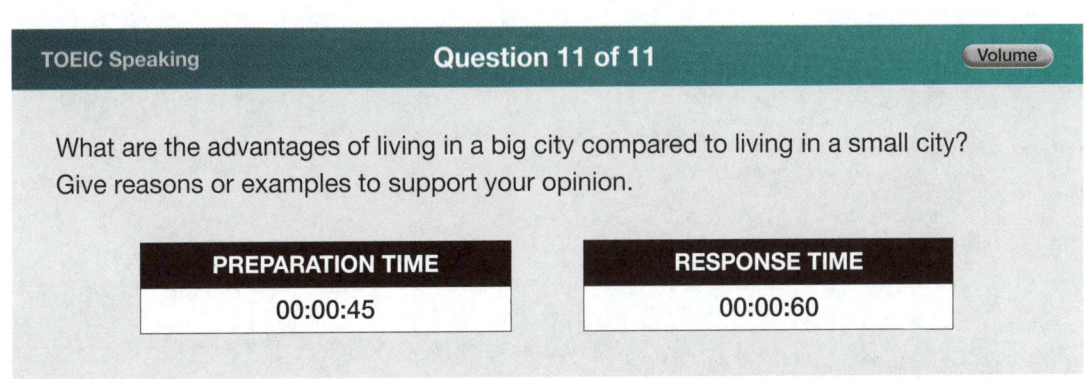

Chapter 3

PART 1
Read a text aloud

PART 2
Describe a picture

PART 3
Respond to questions

PART 4
Respond to questions using information provided

PART 5
Express an opinion

REVIEW TEST 3

PART 1 Read a text aloud

GROUNDWORK

Master The Basics 이론 학습

Background Knowledge 배경 지식

Read the explanations and learn the word stress rules in English.
다음 설명을 읽고 영어의 강세 규칙을 익혀 보세요.

- In English, only one syllable in each word is stressed.
- It's always a vowel, never a consonant.
- It is important to try to feel the sound and rhythm of the language and to add the stress naturally through practice.

Stress on the first syllable

- Most 2-syllable nouns
  - **e.g.** t**a**ble, w**a**ter, p**e**ncil, n**a**pkin, Ch**i**na
- Most 2-syllable adjectives
  - **e.g.** h**a**ppy, sk**i**nny, h**a**ndsome, p**e**rfect, br**o**ken, **u**gly, th**i**rsty

Stress on the last syllable

- Most 2-syllable verbs
  - **e.g.** expl**ai**n, supp**o**rt, disc**u**ss, impr**o**ve, dec**i**de

Stress on the second-from-the-end syllable

- Words ending in "-sion" and "-tion"
  - **e.g.** expl**o**sion, occ**a**sion, dec**i**sion, cond**i**tion, communic**a**tion, prom**o**tion
- Words ending in "-ic"
  - **e.g.** gr**a**phic, scient**i**fic, real**i**stic, spec**i**fic, acad**e**mic, dr**a**stic, pand**e**mic

Stress on the third-from-the-end syllable

- Words ending in "-al"
  - **e.g.** n**a**tural, cr**i**tical, **o**ptional, econ**o**mical, prof**e**ssional
- Words ending in "-ty," "-cy," "-phy," "-gy"
  - **e.g.** respons**i**bility, fac**i**lity, eff**i**ciency, em**e**rgency, phil**o**sophy, techn**o**logy

In the case of compound words

- Compound nouns (stress on the first part)
  - **e.g.** g**e**ntleman, b**o**yfriend, n**e**wspaper, s**e**afood, d**i**shwasher
- Compound verbs (stress on the second part)
  - **e.g.** set **u**p, get thr**o**ugh, take **o**ff, underst**a**nd, figure **o**ut, look f**o**rward to

Type Analysis: News 유형 분석: 뉴스

- News is a text that reports on events through broadcast media, deliver traffic updates, and/or provide weather forecasts.
- It is important to read proper nouns and foreign words with the right English pronunciation and keep your reading speed consistent.

Useful Expressions 유용한 표현

These are the vocabulary and expressions commonly found in the news type texts of PART 1. Try to learn the meanings and pronunciations of each.
다음은 PART 1 지문 유형 중 뉴스 기사문에 자주 쓰이는 어휘 및 표현들입니다. 각각의 뜻을 익혀 보세요.

- weather forecast
  일기 예보
- temperature
  온도
- expected
  예측된
- traffic report
  교통 정보
- southbound
  남행
- roadway
  도로
- alternate routes
  대체 경로
- interstate
  주간 고속 도로
- generate
  생성하다
- industry
  산업
- well-known
  잘 알려진

Practice 적용 연습

Read the given passage with a calm and clear tone of voice while paying attention to the intonation marks.
억양 기호에 주의하며 주어진 지문을 차분하고 분명한 어조로 읽어 보세요.

> It's time for the morning weather report from the Oakland Hills weather station. ↘ It will be sunny most of the day, with temperatures remaining below twenty-five degrees Celsius. However, things will change tomorrow. We're expecting light winds, ↗ rainfall, ↗ and humidity. ↘ So, if you plan to be outside tomorrow, remember to take your umbrella.

MINI TEST

🎧 C3 P1 Mini Test, C3 P1 Model Answer

TOEIC Speaking   **Question 1 of 11**   Volume

In local news, the owner of China Palace announced that his restaurants will now only use vegetables grown locally. This means that most of the greens, tomatoes, and onions on their dishes will come from farms around Hayward. Although the owner is aware that this change will cost the company thirty percent more, he is firmly committed to supporting local farmers.

PREPARATION TIME	RESPONSE TIME
00:00:45	00:00:45

Translation 해석

현지 뉴스를 통해 China Palace의 소유주는 앞으로 자신의 식당에서 현지 재배한 채소만 사용할 것이라고 밝혔습니다. 이는 해당 식당의 메뉴를 구성하는 대부분의 녹색 채소, 토마토, 그리고 양파를 Hayward 주변의 농장들로부터 수급한다는 것을 의미합니다. 소유주는 해당 변화로 인해 30% 정도의 추가 비용이 발생한다는 것을 알고 있음에도 불구하고, 지역 농가를 지지하는 데 전념하고 있습니다.

TOEIC Speaking   Question 2 of 11

And now for the radio traffic report from News Eleven. Construction on Geary Street is affecting drivers this afternoon. Westbound lanes, bicycle lanes, and sidewalks are all blocked as workers repave parts of the street. Since the work is expected until 6 p.m., travelers should consider taking alternate routes.

PREPARATION TIME	RESPONSE TIME
00:00:45	00:00:45

Translation 해석

이번 순서는 News Eleven의 라디오 교통 정보입니다. Geary Street에서 진행 중인 공사가 오늘 오후 운전자들에게 영향을 주고 있습니다. 도로의 일부를 재포장함에 따라 서쪽으로 향하는 차선, 자전거 도로, 그리고 인도의 통행이 모두 차단됩니다. 오후 6시까지 작업이 이어질 것으로 예상되므로, 이동하시는 분들은 다른 경로를 고려해 보셔야겠습니다.

PART 2 Describe a picture

GROUNDWORK

📍 Type Analysis: Street 유형 분석: 길거리

Useful Expression 유용한 표현

These are the vocabulary and expressions that can be used when describing a picture taken on a street in PART 2. Try to learn the meanings and pronunciations of each.
다음은 PART 2 사진 유형 중 거리에서 찍힌 사진을 묘사할 때 유용하게 쓸 수 있는 어휘 및 표현들입니다. 각각의 뜻을 익혀 보세요.

- sidewalk
  인도
- traffic light
  신호등
- crosswalk
  횡단보도
- traffic sign
  도로 표지판
- brick wall
  벽돌 담

- structure
  건축물, 구조물
- well-maintained
  잘 관리되어 있는
- decorated
  장식된
- crowded
  붐비는
- busy [quiet] street
  바쁜 [한산한] 거리

- traffic congestion
  교통 체증
- cross the street
  길을 건너다
- pass by
  ~을 지나가다
- stand in a line
  일렬로 서다
- overcast
  구름이 덮인, 흐린

- vendor
  상인
- signboard
  간판
- parked along the street
  거리를 따라 주차되어 있는
- walk in different directions
  다른 방향으로 걷다

Sample Practice 예제 연습

> **Ideation**
>
> Look at the picture and think about what you want to focus on when describing it.
> 다음 사진을 보고, 무엇을 묘사할 것인지 생각해 보세요.

- Where do you think this picture was taken?
- What's the first thing you see in this picture?
- What do you think the weather is like?
- Can you guess what time it is by looking at this picture?
- What do you see on both sides of the picture?
- What do you feel when you look at the picture?

Answer Structure

Now, follow the steps below to organize your response systematically.
이제, 아래 단계에 따라 답변을 체계적으로 구성해 보세요.

STEP 1 Place & Number of people

Begin by stating the location where the picture might have been taken. If possible, also mention the number of people in the picture.

Pattern 1
This picture was taken _____.
- on a street • on a busy city street

Pattern 2
I see _____ people in this picture.
- many • a lot of

STEP 2 Main person or thing

Describe the main person or thing in the picture.

Pattern
The first thing I'm noticing is _____.
- many people crossing the street
- many people walking in different directions

STEP 3 Surroundings

Say a few things about the rest of the picture by using location descriptions.

Pattern
Behind them, _____.
- I see a lot of cars stuck in traffic
- there are tall buildings standing along the street

STEP 4 Opinions or feelings about the picture

Conclude by expressing your thoughts or feelings about the picture.

Pattern 1
It seems like _____.
- a typical scene from a busy street

Pattern 2
I like/don't like this picture because _____.
- it reminds me of my hometown

MINI TEST

C3 P2 Mini Test

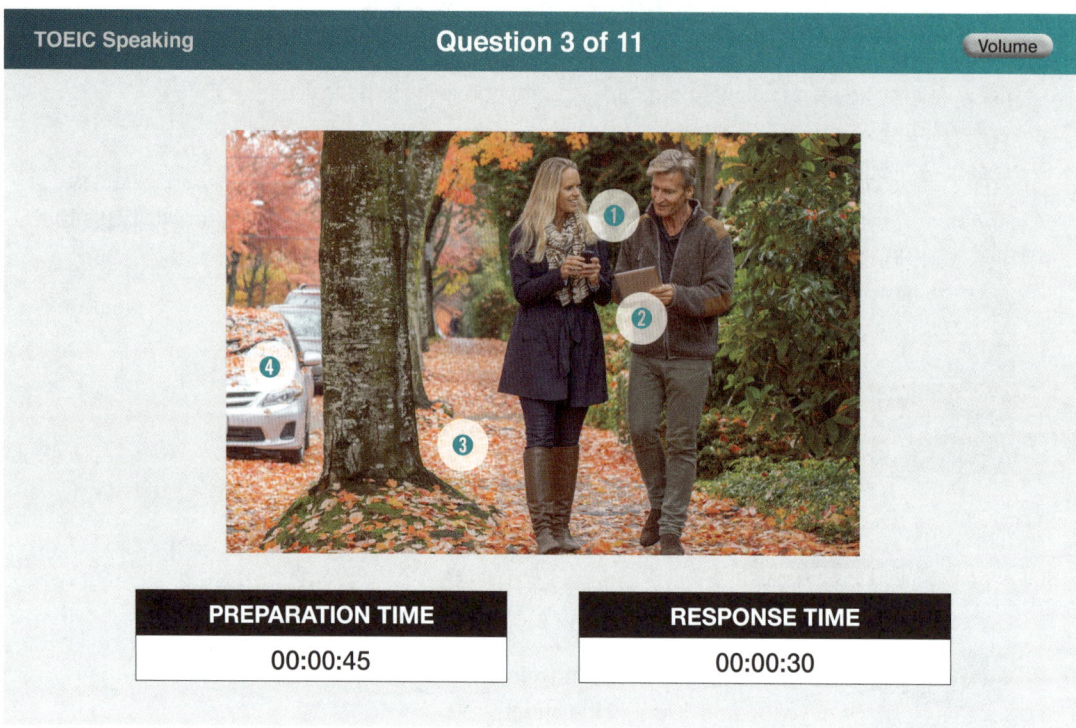

HINT 1 Answer Structure 답변 구조

This picture was taken on a sidewalk.

❶ The first thing I notice is _____.

❷ The man is _____, and the woman is _____.

❸ There are _____. By looking at the _____.

❹ On the left, _____.

I like this picture because it's very peaceful.

HINT 2 Useful Expression 유용한 표현

- sidewalk
  인도, 보행자 도로
- fallen leaves
  낙엽
- stand in a line
  일렬로 서다
- chilly weather
  쌀쌀한 날씨
- parked along the street
  길가에 주차되어 있는
- walk in the same direction
  같은 방향으로 걷다
- walk together
  함께 걷다
- have a conversation
  대화를 나누다

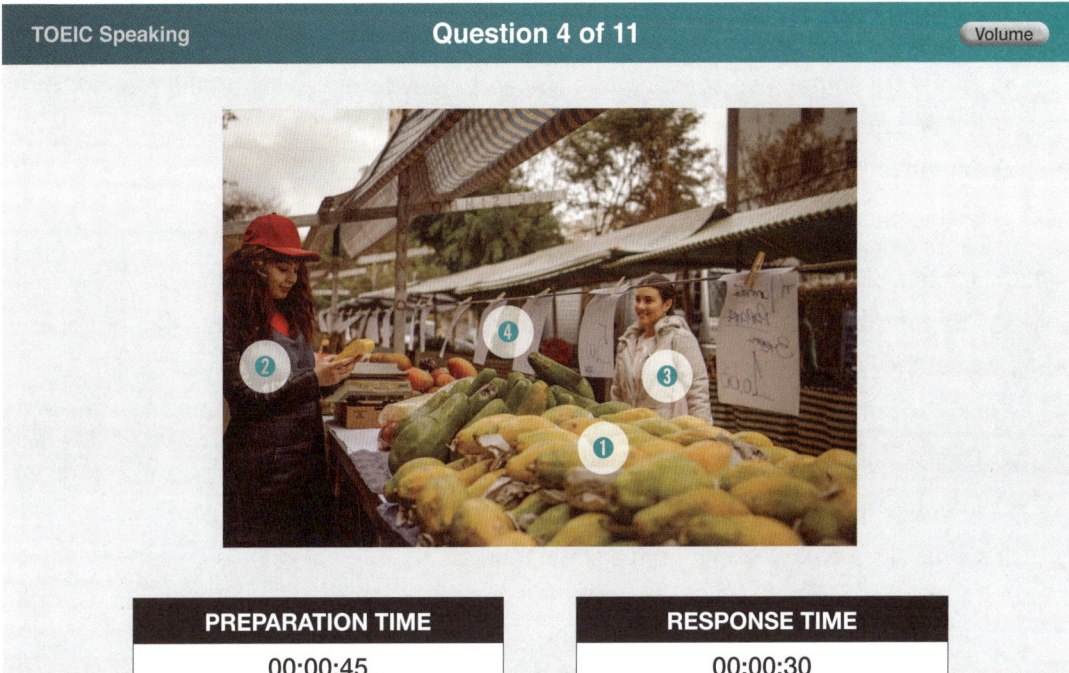

HINT 1 Answer Structure 답변 구조

I think this picture was taken at a street market.

❶ The first thing I notice is _____.

❷ On the left, _____.

❸ On the right, _____.

❹ In between them, _____.

It seems like a typical scene from a street market.

HINT 2 Useful Expression 유용한 표현

- street market
  길거리 시장
- price tag
  가격표
- food product
  식료품
- stacked up
  쌓여 있는
- wavy hair
  웨이브가 진 머리
- seem to be
  ~인 것 같다
- employee
  직원
- make a purchase
  구매하다

Chapter 3 PART 2 Describe a picture 87

Model Answer 모범 답안

🎧 C3 P2 Model Answer

3. This picture was taken on a sidewalk.

   ❶ **The first thing I notice is** a man and a woman walking together on the sidewalk.

   ❷ **The man is** holding a tablet PC, **and the woman is** holding a smartphone.

   ❸ **There are** some trees standing in a line and many fallen leaves on the ground. **By looking at the** colors of the leaves, I can tell that it's the fall season.

   ❹ **On the left,** I can see some cars parked along the street.

   I like this picture because it's giving me a very peaceful vibe.

4. I think this picture was taken at a street market.

   ❶ **The first thing I notice is** many food items stacked up on the table. I'm not sure what they are, but they seem to be some sort of fruits and vegetables.

   ❷ **On the left,** a woman wearing a red hat is helping a customer.

   ❸ **On the right,** the customer is standing with a smile on her face.

   ❹ **In between them,** I can see many price tags hung up on a line.

   It seems like a typical scene from a street market.

Translation 해석

3. 이 사진은 보행자 도로에서 찍힌 사진입니다.
   ❶ 가장 먼저 눈에 띄는 것은 함께 보행자 도로를 걷고 있는 한 남성과 여성입니다.
   ❷ 남자는 태블릿 PC를 들고 있고 여자는 스마트폰을 들고 있습니다.
   ❸ 몇 그루의 나무가 일렬로 서 있고 땅에는 낙엽이 많이 떨어져 있습니다. 낙엽의 색깔을 보니 가을임을 알 수 있습니다.
   ❹ 왼쪽에는 길을 따라 주차되어 있는 자동차들이 보입니다.
   저는 이 사진이 매우 평화로운 느낌을 주기 때문에 좋습니다.

4. 이 사진은 길거리 시장에서 찍힌 것 같습니다.
   ❶ 가장 먼저 눈에 띄는 것은 테이블 위에 쌓여 있는 많은 식품입니다. 그것들이 무엇인지 잘 모르겠지만 일종의 과일들과 채소들인 것 같습니다.
   ❷ 왼쪽에는 빨간 모자를 쓴 여성이 고객을 응대하고 있습니다.
   ❸ 오른쪽에는 고객이 미소를 띤 채 서 있습니다.
   ❹ 그들 사이에는 줄에 걸려 있는 많은 가격표들이 보입니다.
   길거리 시장의 전형적인 풍경처럼 보입니다.

PART 3 Respond to questions

GROUNDWORK

📍 Master The Basics 이론 학습

Background Knowledge 배경 지식

You can answer the questions of PART 3 by explaining your emotions and feelings. We will now learn some patterns that show positive and negative emotions. Try to use them to extend your answer.

여러분의 감정을 소재로 하여 PART 3의 질문들에 답변할 수 있습니다. 이번 단원에서는 긍정적 또는 부정적 감정을 표현하는 패턴을 익히고 이를 답변에 활용하는 연습을 할 것입니다.

Positive Emotion & Feeling

You can talk about how you feel about what you're asked by using the sentences as follows:
- It gives me energy.
- It helps me relieve stress.
- It makes me feel excited/happy/great.
- It's relaxing/mentally refreshing.

e.g.

Question: Do you enjoy outdoor activities? Why or why not?
Answer: Yes, I enjoy outdoor activities. That's because it helps relieve stress and makes me feel great.

Negative Emotion & Feeling

If you want to talk about a negative side of what you're asked, you can use the sentences as follows:
- It drains my energy.
- It stresses me out. / It's very stressful.
- It makes me feel sad. / It makes me feel down.
- It's mentally exhausting.

e.g.

Question: Do you enjoy outdoor activities? Why or why not?
Answer: No, I don't enjoy outdoor activities. That's because it drains my energy.

Practice 적용 연습

Based on what you have learned, practice answering the following questions.
학습한 내용을 바탕으로, 다음 질문에 답변해 보세요.

Question

1. **Question**: What kind of music do you enjoy listening to? Why?
   Answer: I enjoy listening to _____ . That's because _____ .

2. **Question**: What device do you usually use to listen to music?
   Answer: I usually use _____ . That's because _____ .

3. **Question**: Do you think listening to music is a good way to spend your free time?
   Answer:
   - **Topic sentence** _____ .
   - **Time killer** _____ .
   - **Reason 1** First of all, _____ .
   - **Reason 2** Moreover, _____ .
   - **Wrap up** Considering these factors, _____ .

Model Answer

1. jazz music, it's very relaxing
2. the audio system at home, the sound quality is great and it helps me relieve stress
3.
   - **Topic sentence** I believe that listening to music is a great way to spend my free time
   - **Time killer** There are several reasons to support my opinion
   - **Reason 1** listening to music helps reduce stress
   - **Reason 2** it boosts my energy, especially when I listen to upbeat songs
   - **Wrap up** I think listening to music is a good way to spend my free time

MINI TEST

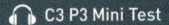

C3 P3 Mini Test

TOEIC Speaking Question 5 of 11 Volume

Imagine a consulting firm is conducting research about taking breaks during work or school. You have agreed to participate in a telephone interview about taking breaks.

How many breaks do you usually take in a day? And when do you usually take your first break?

PREPARATION TIME	RESPONSE TIME
00:00:03	00:00:15

TOEIC Speaking Question 6 of 11 Volume

Imagine a consulting firm is conducting research about taking breaks during work or school. You have agreed to participate in a telephone interview about taking breaks.

How long do your breaks typically last? And do you usually take your breaks alone?

PREPARATION TIME	RESPONSE TIME
00:00:03	00:00:15

TOEIC Speaking Question 7 of 11 Volume

Imagine a consulting firm is conducting research about taking breaks during work or school. You have agreed to participate in a telephone interview about taking breaks.

What is your favorite thing to do during your break time? Why?

PREPARATION TIME	RESPONSE TIME
00:00:03	00:00:30

Model Answer 모범 답안

C3 P3 Model Answer

5. I usually take two breaks a day. And I usually take my first break at noon, which is my lunch time.

6. My breaks typically last about an hour. And I usually take my breaks alone because I don't want to be disturbed.

7.
- **Topic sentence** — My favorite thing to do during break times is going on walks.
- **Time killer** — I have a few reasons why.
- **Reason 1** — First of all, walking helps relieve my stress. I feel better after a good walk.
- **Reason 2** — Also, I believe it's good for my health and gives me positive energy.
- **Wrap up** — That's why my favorite thing to do during my break time is going on walks.

Translation 해석

상황 설정
한 컨설팅 회사가 직장 또는 학교에서 휴식을 취하는 것에 대한 연구를 수행하는 중이라고 가정해 봅시다. 여러분은 휴식을 취하는 것과 관련해 유선 설문 조사에 응하기로 했습니다.

5번 질문, 모범 답안
Q: 하루에 보통 몇 번 휴식하시나요? 그리고 보통 언제 첫 휴식 시간을 가지시나요?
A: 저는 보통 하루에 두 번 쉽니다. 첫 휴식 시간은 정오에 갖는데요, 그때가 제 점심 시간이기 때문입니다.

6번 질문, 모범 답안
Q: 일반적으로 휴식 시간은 얼마나 가지시나요? 그리고 보통 혼자 휴식을 취하시나요?
A: 제 휴식 시간은 보통 한 시간 정도 됩니다. 그리고 저는 휴식 시간이 방해 받기를 원하지 않아서 주로 혼자 쉬는 편이에요.

7번 질문, 모범 답안
Q: 휴식 시간에 가장 즐겨하는 것은 무엇입니까? 왜 그렇죠?
A:
- **Topic sentence** — 휴식 시간에 제가 가장 즐겨하는 것은 산책하는 것입니다.
- **Time killer** — 몇 가지 이유가 있습니다.
- **Reason 1** — 우선, 걷기는 스트레스 해소에 도움이 됩니다. 산책을 잘 하고 나면 기분이 좋아집니다.
- **Reason 2** — 또한, 저는 산책이 건강에 좋으며 저에게 긍정적인 기운을 준다고 생각합니다.
- **Wrap up** — 그것이 제가 휴식 시간에 산책을 가장 즐겨하는 이유입니다.

PART 4 Respond to questions using information provided

GROUNDWORK

📍 Master The Basics 이론 학습

Background Knowledge 배경 지식

In PART 4, correctly reading numbers and dates in a schedule is essential. Learn how to read numbers and dates in each case and practice reading them.
PART 4에서는 특히 일정과 관련된 숫자와 날짜를 올바르게 읽는 것이 중요합니다. 각 경우에 숫자를 어떻게 읽어야 하는지 학습해 보고, 소리 내어 읽는 연습을 해 보세요.

Month

Here is the name of each month. In particular, pay attention to the pronunciations of "January," "February," and "August" which many Koreans get confused about.

- January
- February
- March
- April
- May
- June
- July
- August
- September
- October
- November
- December

Dates

When talking about dates, you should pronounce numbers in their ordinal form. For your information, on days 13-19, pronounce the "teenth" long. Also, be sure to pronounce 5th correctly. While paying special attention to those tips, read the following numbers aloud.

- 1st first
- 2nd second
- 3rd third
- 4th fourth
- 5th fifth
- 6th sixth
- 7th seventh
- 8th eighth
- 9th ninth
- 10th tenth
- 11th eleventh
- 12th twelfth
- 13th thirteenth
- 14th fourteenth
- 15th fifteenth
- 16th sixteenth
- 17th seventeenth
- 18th eighteenth
- 19th nineteenth
- 20th twentieth
- 21st twenty-first
- 22nd twenty-second
- 23rd twenty-third
- 24th twenty-fourth
- 25th twenty-fifth
- 26th twenty-sixth
- 27th twenty-seventh
- 28th twenty-eighth
- 29th twenty-ninth
- 30th thirtieth
- 31st thirty-first

Days

When talking about the day an event is held on, there is a chance that you have to pronounce the name of the day. While paying attention to the spelling and pronunciation of each name, read the following texts aloud.

- Monday
- Tuesday
- Wednesday
- Thursday
- Friday
- Saturday
- Sunday

Time

When talking about hours and minutes, it's also essential to ensure you are reading the numbers correctly. Also, in PART 4, 12 p.m. is often referred to as "noon," so be careful not to confuse its meaning.

- 9 a.m. nine a.m
- 6:15 p.m. six fifteen p.m.
- noon ~ 2:30 p.m. from noon to two thirty p.m.

Practice 적용 연습

Based on what you have learned, answer the following questions.
학습한 내용을 바탕으로, 다음 질문에 답변해 보세요.

Question

1. What's today's date?
2. When is your birthday?
3. When is Christmas?
4. When is your father's birthday?
5. Which day of the week do you hate the most?
6. Which month is your favorite month of the year?
7. What time do you usually go to bed in the evenings? And what time do you usually get up in the mornings?

Model Answer

1. It's August twenty-third, two thousand twenty-three.
2. I was born in March nineteenth, nineteen ninety-nine.
3. December twenty-fifth is Christmas Day.
4. His birthday is September eighth.
5. I hate Wednesdays the most because they're right in the middle of the week.
6. February is my favorite month of the year because the Korean Lunar New Year's Day usually happens in February.
7. I usually go to bed at ten p.m. and wake up at 7 in the morning.

MINI TEST

🎧 C3 P4 Mini Test

TOEIC Speaking Question 8-10 of 11   Volume

Franklin Library
Meeting Room Schedule
- Jan. ~ Mar. (Updated) -

Club / Group	Day of the Week	Time
Book Club: Mystery Novels	Mondays	5:00 ~ 6:00 p.m.
Poetry Reading Group	Tuesdays	6:00 ~ 7:00 p.m.
Essay Writing Club (Junior High School)	Wednesdays	4:30 ~ 5:30 p.m.
Children's Story Time (All Ages)	Thursdays	1:00 ~ 1:30 p.m.
Franklin Neighborhood Community	Fridays	6:00 ~ 8:00 p.m.
Essay Writing Club (High School)	Saturdays	Noon ~ 1:30 p.m.

- Hours of Operation: Noon ~ 8:00 p.m.
- Reservation: Please contact the library a week in advance.

PREPARATION TIME
00:00:45

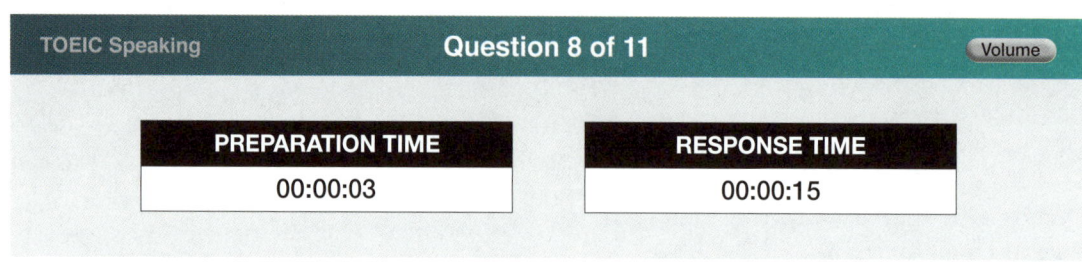

「HINT Useful Expression 유용한 표현
- day of the week 요일
- meet 모이다
- from A to B A부터 B까지

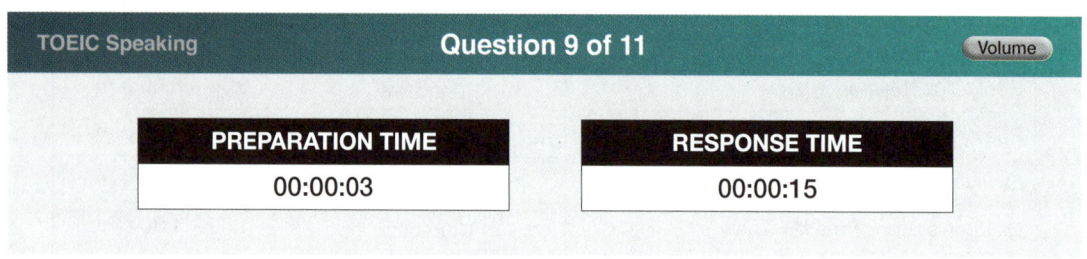

「HINT Useful Expression 유용한 표현
- I am afraid that … 유감이지만 …입니다
- actually 사실은
- be scheduled on ~에 일정이 잡혀 있다

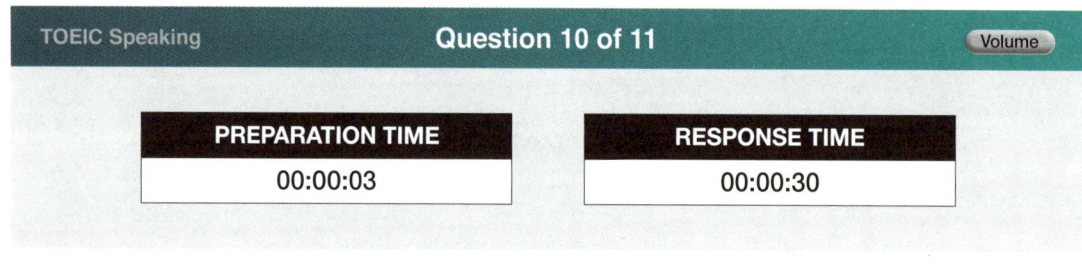

「HINT Useful Expression 유용한 표현
- make changes 변경하다
- detail 자세한 사항
- another 또 다른

Model Answer 모범 답안

C3 P4 Model Answer

Franklin Library
Meeting Room Schedule
- Jan. ~ Mar. (Updated) -

Club / Group	Day of the Week	Time
Book Club: Mystery Novels	Mondays	5:00 ~ 6:00 p.m.
❽ Poetry Reading Group	Tuesdays	6:00 ~ 7:00 p.m.
❿ Essay Writing Club (Junior High School)	Wednesdays	4:30 ~ 5:30 p.m.
Children's Story Time (All Ages)	Thursdays	1:00 ~ 1:30 p.m.
❾ Franklin Neighborhood Community	Fridays	6:00 ~ 8:00 p.m.
❿ Essay Writing Club (High School)	Saturdays	Noon ~ 1:30 p.m.

- Hours of Operation: Noon ~ 8:00 p.m.
- Reservation: Please contact the library a week in advance.

Narration: Hi, this is Jenny, the library director. I heard that the schedule for the group meeting rooms has just been updated, and I wanted to confirm some details.

8. Question: What days of the week will the Poetry Reading Group meet, and what time will their meeting start?
Answer: The Poetry Reading Group will meet on Tuesdays from 6 to 7 p.m.

9. Question: The Franklin Neighborhood Community will meet on Thursdays, right?
Answer: Actually, you have the wrong information. The Franklin Neighborhood Community will meet on Fridays from 6 to 8 p.m.

10. Question: I know some changes were made to the Essay Writing Club. Can you tell me all the details you have about the Essay Writing Club?
Answer: Sure. There are two scheduled essay writing clubs. First, the Essay Writing Club for Junior High School will meet on Wednesdays from 4:30 to 5:30 p.m. Also, another Essay Writing Club for High School will meet on Saturdays from noon to 1:30 p.m.

Translation 해석

나레이션
안녕하십니까. 도서관장 Jenny입니다. 회의실 대여 일정이 업데이트 되었다고 들었습니다. 몇 가지 세부 사항을 확인하고 싶네요.

8번 질문, 모범 답안
Q: 시 읽기 모임은 무슨 요일에 모이며 몇시에 시작합니까?
A: 시 읽기 모임은 매주 화요일 오후 6시부터 7시까지 모입니다.

9번 질문, 모범 답안
Q: Franklin 지역 주민회는 목요일에 모이는 것 맞나요?
A: 사실 잘못된 정보를 알고 계십니다. Franklin 지역 주민회는 매주 금요일 오후 6시부터 8시까지 모입니다.

10번 질문, 모범 답안
Q: 에세이 쓰기 클럽에 약간의 변동이 있었던 것으로 알고 있습니다. 에세이 쓰기 클럽에 대해 알고 있는 모든 세부 사항을 말씀해 주시겠습니까?
A: 물론이죠. 에세이 쓰기 클럽 관련 일정이 두 가지 있는데요. 우선 중학 에세이 쓰기 클럽은 매주 수요일 4시 30분부터 5시 30분까지 모입니다. 또한 고등 에세이 쓰기 클럽은 매주 토요일 정오부터 오후 1시 30분까지 모입니다.

PART 5

Express an opinion

GROUNDWORK

◉ Type Analysis: Choice-making 유형 분석: 선택형 질문

Background Knowledge 배경 지식

We will now take a look at the "choice-making" question types. Follow the same answer sequence we have learned in the previous chapters for these question types.

이번 단원에서는 여러 선택지를 제시하고 그 중 무엇을 고를 것인지 묻는 '선택형' 질문에 답변하는 방법을 연습할 것입니다. 이전 단원들에서 학습했던 답변 구조를 이 유형의 질문에도 적용해 볼 수 있습니다.

Question Example

Which of the following do you think contributes the most to a person's success?

Choose ONE of the options provided below and give specific reasons or examples to support your opinion.

- Natural talent
- Luck
- Hard work

Answer Structure

Keep the following order in mind to respond to the question in a more organized manner.
다음 순서에 유념하여 답변을 논리적으로 구성해 보세요.

STEP 1 Choose an option

For "choice-making" question types, remember to choose one of the options and use the expression in the question to start off your first sentence.

| Expression to use | • I think _____ .
 • I would say _____ . |

e.g. I would say natural talent contributes the most to a person's success.

STEP 2 — Explain your reasons

Explain your reasons for your choice using the following expressions.

Expression to use
- The main reason is that _____.
- Secondly, _____.

e.g. **The main reason is that** if a person has natural talent in his or her field, they wouldn't have to work or think as hard and still get the results they want. **Secondly,** I don't believe in luck because it's not reliable.

STEP 3 — Support your reasons using examples

Use your own experience as an example to support your claims. It doesn't affect the score if the examples are not true.

Expression to use
- When I was young, _____.
- For many years, _____.

e.g. **When I was young,** my best friend and I started to learn how to play golf together. I quickly noticed that my friend had natural talent, and I could never beat him. He eventually became a professional golfer.

STEP 4 — Conclude

Finish your response by summarizing the argument.

Expression to use
- That is why I think _____.

e.g. **That is why I think** natural talent contributes the most to a person's success.

Practice 적용 연습

Based on what you have learned, answer the following questions.
학습한 내용을 바탕으로, 다음 질문에 답변해 보세요.

Question

Which of the following do you think affects the success of a business the most? Choose ONE of the options provided below and give reasons or examples to support your opinion.

- Customer service
- Quality of product
- Advertising

HINT 1 Answer Structure 답변 구조

STEP 1 Choose an option
I think _____ affects the success of a business the most.

STEP 2 Explain your reasons
- The main reason is that _____.
- Secondly, _____.

STEP 3 Support your reasons using examples
- For instance, _____.
- From my experience, _____.

STEP 4 Conclude
That's why I think _____ affects the success of a business the most.

HINT 2 Useful Expression 유용한 표현

- satisfaction 만족
- customer loyalty 고객 충성도
- business asset 사업 자산
- long-term 장기적인
- attract customers 고객을 유치하다
- retain 유지하다
- competitive advantage 경쟁 우위
- competitor 경쟁자, 경쟁업체
- expectation 기대
- revenue 수익
- better reputation 더 나은 평판
- word of mouth 입소문

Model Answer

STEP 1 I think customer service affects the success of a business the most.

STEP 2 The main reason is that excellent customer service can be a key differentiator in today's competitive market.
Secondly, good customer service can lead to customer satisfaction and retention. Maintaining customers can contribute to long-term success and growth of a business.

STEP 3 For instance, I've been a loyal customer of Samsung because of their excellent customer care.

STEP 4 That's why I think customer service affects the success of a business the most.

MINI TEST

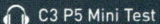

C3 P5 Mini Test

TOEIC Speaking Question 11 of 11 Volume

Which of the following skills do you think is the most important for a business leader? Choose ONE of the options provided below and give reasons or examples to support your opinion.
- Risk management skills
- Financial literacy
- Emotional intelligence

PREPARATION TIME	RESPONSE TIME
00:00:45	00:00:60

HINT ANSWER STRUCTURE

STEP 1 I would say _____ is(are) the most important skill(s) for a business leader.
STEP 1 • The main reason is that _____.
  • Secondly, _____.
STEP 3 • In my case, _____.
  • For the last several years, _____.
STEP 4 That's why I think _____.

Model Answer 모범 답안

🎧 C3 P5 Model Answer

STEP 1 I would say financial literacy is the most important skill for a business leader.

STEP 2 • The main reason is that the essence of business is to make profits, and to achieve this, effective financial management is essential.
• Secondly, by demonstrating effective financial management, one can gain the trust of team members.

STEP 3 In my case, the CEO of my previous company had overspent on employee benefits, leading the company to financial difficulties. He lost the trust of the employees, and many of them left the company.

STEP 4 That's why I think financial literacy is the most essential ability for a business leader.

Translation 해석

문제
다음 중 경영인이 갖추어야 할 역량으로 가장 중요한 것이 무엇이라고 생각하십니까?
보기 중 하나를 골라 구체적인 근거 또는 사례를 들어 의견을 뒷받침하십시오.
- 위기 관리 역량
- 재정 분야에 대한 지식
- 감성 지능

모범 답안

STEP 1 저는 재정 분야에 대한 지식이 **경영인에게 가장 필요한 역량이라고 생각합니다.**

STEP 2 • **왜냐하면** 사업의 본질은 수익을 내는 것이고, 이를 달성하기 위해서는 효과적인 재정 관리가 필수적이기 때문입니다.
• 또한, 효과적인 재정 관리 능력을 보여줌으로써 경영자는 직원들의 신임을 얻을 수 있습니다.

STEP 3 저의 경우, 이전 직장의 대표님께서 직원 복지에 너무 많은 지출을 하는 바람에 회사가 재정난을 겪은 적이 있습니다. 당시 대표님은 직원들의 신임을 잃었고, 많은 직원들이 회사를 떠났습니다.

STEP 4 이것이 제가 재정 분야에 대한 지식이 경영인에게 가장 중요한 능력이라고 생각하는 **이유입니다.**

REVIEW TEST 3

TOEIC Speaking Question 1 of 11 Volume

Good evening, and welcome to Channel Six News. This spring, the city of Fullerton will welcome hundreds of visitors for the historic car festival. In addition to the car show, local vendors will be offering food, drinks, and other refreshments. If the rumors are correct, we can even expect a few celebrity appearances. Stay tuned for more details.

PREPARATION TIME	RESPONSE TIME
00:00:45	00:00:45

TOEIC Speaking Question 2 of 11 Volume

Good afternoon, and thank you for listening to local radio news. Today, we'll bring you stories about upcoming elections, the new parking meter system, and renovations to the university library. After that, stay tuned for the Top Ten local sports. To see video coverage of any of our featured stories, you can visit our website.

PREPARATION TIME	RESPONSE TIME
00:00:45	00:00:45

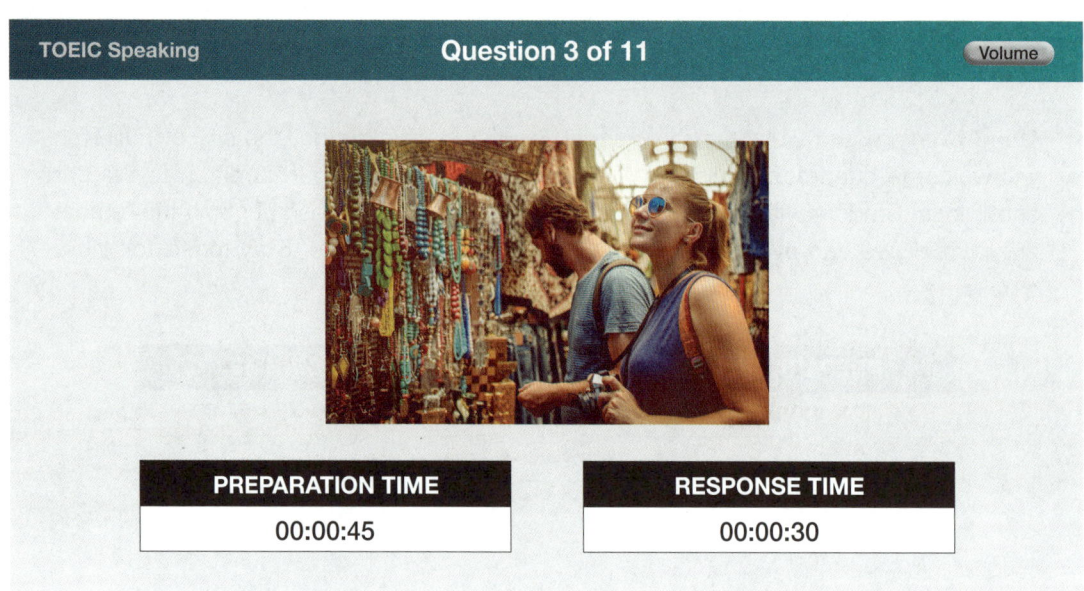

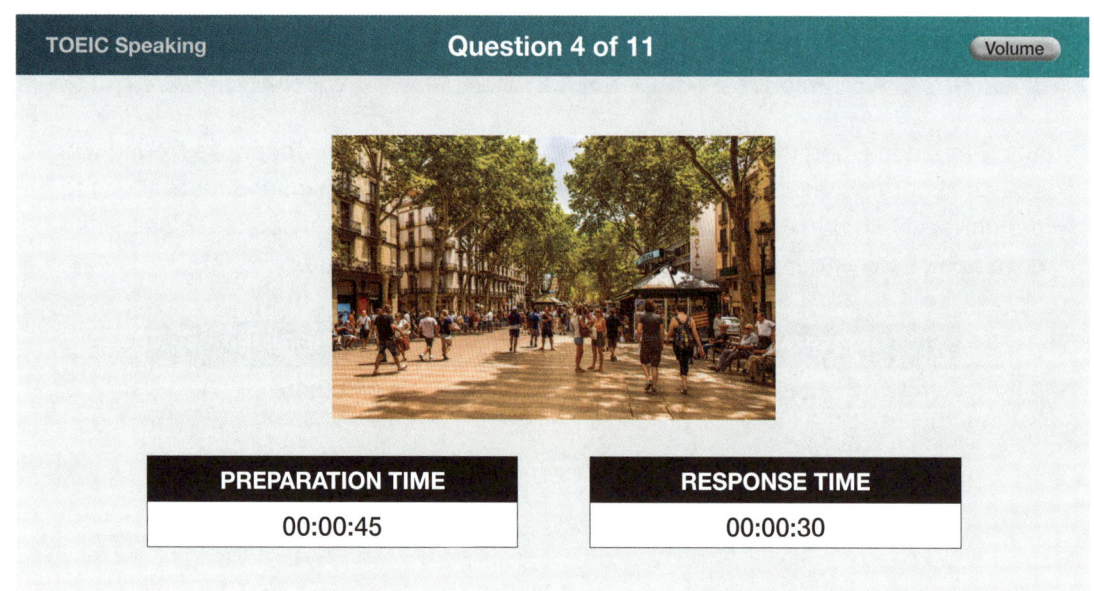

TOEIC Speaking	Question 5 of 11	

Imagine that a university professor is doing research in your area. You have agreed to participate in a telephone interview about festivals.

When was the last time you went to a festival, and what kind of festival was it?

PREPARATION TIME	RESPONSE TIME
00:00:03	00:00:15

TOEIC Speaking	Question 6 of 11	

Imagine that a university professor is doing research in your area. You have agreed to participate in a telephone interview about festivals.

Do you prefer to go to a festival when it's free of admission, or when you have to pay for it?

PREPARATION TIME	RESPONSE TIME
00:00:03	00:00:15

TOEIC Speaking	Question 7 of 11	

Imagine that a university professor is doing research in your area. You have agreed to participate in a telephone interview about festivals.

Which festival do you think is better? A day-time festival or a night-time festival? Why?

PREPARATION TIME	RESPONSE TIME
00:00:03	00:00:30

TOEIC Speaking   Question 8-10 of 11

Napa Film Festival
Schedule for Saturday, Feb. 14
Tickets: $12/film

Starting time	Film title	Location	Genre
3:00 p.m.	*Hangman*	Emeryville Theater	Comedy
3:00 p.m.	*Forever Gone*	Richmond Arts Center	Drama
5:30 p.m.	*The Next Train*	Emeryville Theater	Comedy
5:30 p.m.	*Not My Taste*	Perkin's Theater	Comedy
7:00 p.m.	*Mysteries of Ganges*	Richmond Arts Center	Documentary
7:00 p.m.	*In This Lifetime*	Emeryville Theater	Drama
8:30 p.m.	*The Sea Adventure*	Perkin's Theater	Documentary

PREPARATION TIME
00:00:45

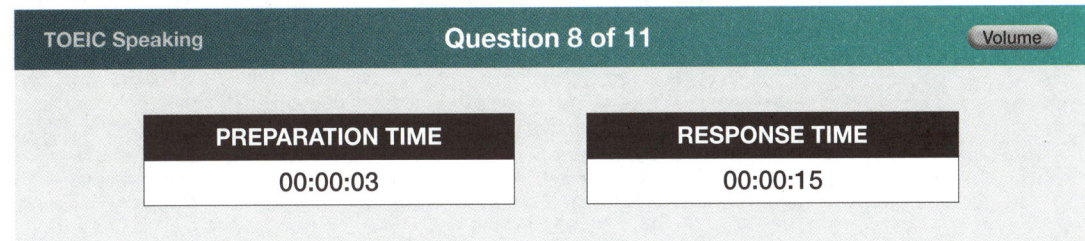

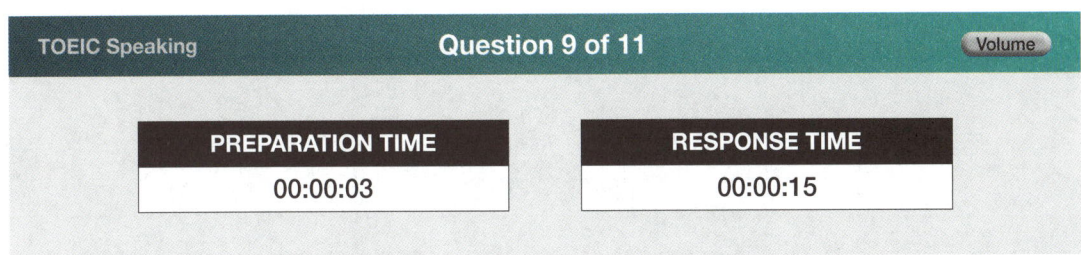

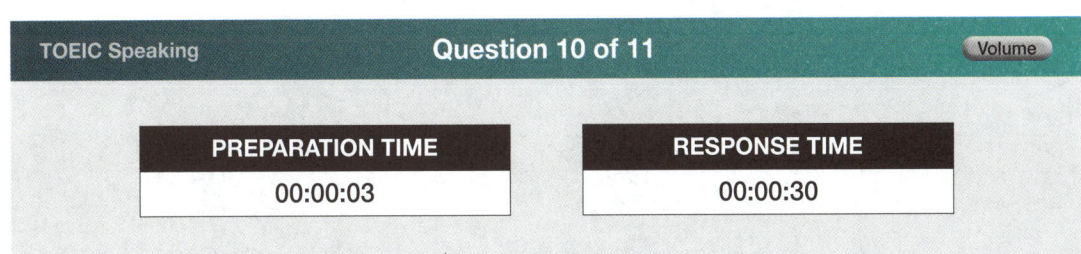

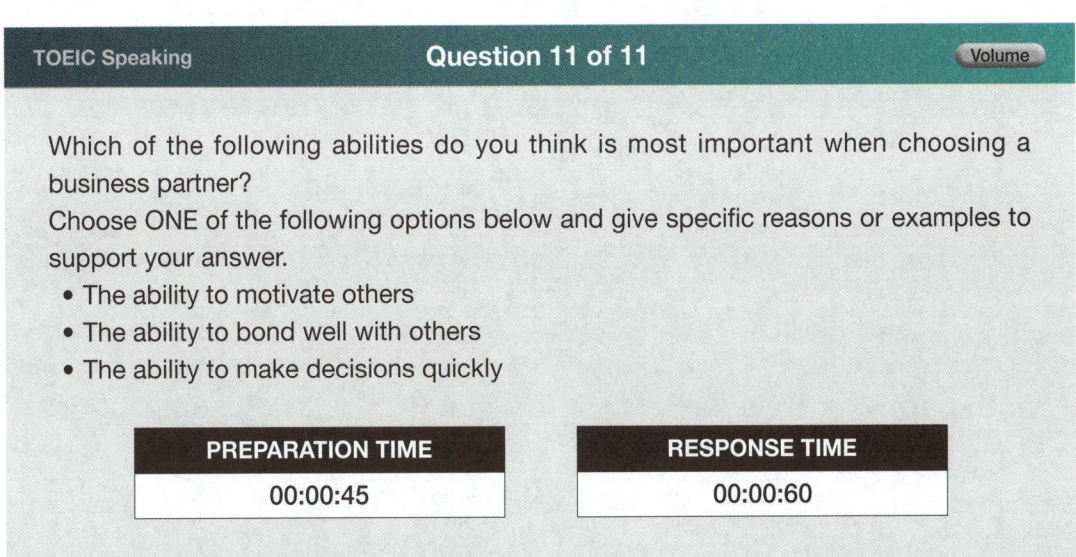

Which of the following abilities do you think is most important when choosing a business partner?
Choose ONE of the following options below and give specific reasons or examples to support your answer.
- The ability to motivate others
- The ability to bond well with others
- The ability to make decisions quickly

Chapter 4

- **PART 1** Read a text aloud
- **PART 2** Describe a picture
- **PART 3** Respond to questions
- **PART 4** Respond to questions using information provided
- **PART 5** Express an opinion

REVIEW TEST 4

PART 1 Read a text aloud

GROUNDWORK

📍 Master The Basics 이론 학습

Background Knowledge 배경 지식

Read the explanations and learn the word stress rules in English.
다음 설명을 읽고 영어의 강세 규칙을 익혀 보세요.

- Intonation is the way the voice rises or falls when communicating.
- Korean is a monotone language, whereas English has multiple tones.
- When communicating in English, sentences may vary in meaning depending on the intonation.
- Sentences sound more compelling when the proper intonation is used.

Falling Intonation

Falling Intonation is one of the most common intonation patterns. They're commonly used in statements and commands.

- Statements
  - e.g. Your call is important to us. ↘
- Commands
  - e.g. Please hold the line. ↘

Rising Intonation

Rising Intonation is when the pitch of the voice rises at the end of the sentence. They're commonly used in yes or no questions and question tags that show uncertainty.

- Yes or no question
  - e.g. Do you like coffee? ↗
- Question tags showing uncertainty
  - e.g. You prefer coke, don't you? ↗

Rising-falling Intonation

Rising-falling intonation is generally used for giving out lists and conditional statements. In PART 1, rising-Falling Intonation will 100% appear on the test.

- Giving out a list
  - e.g. He ordered pizza, ↗ pasta, ↗ and salad. ↘
- Conditional statements
  - e.g. Ever since the road was repaved, ↗ there have been fewer accidents. ↘

Type Analysis: ARS Message 유형 분석: 자동 응답 메시지

- ARS message is a text that provides general information through an automated machine at a certain facility.
- It is important to read with proper intonation in order to convey the message accurately.
- Make sure the tone of your voice is cheerful and tender.

Useful Expressions 유용한 표현

These are the vocabulary and expressions commonly found in the ARS message type texts of PART 1. Try to learn the meanings and pronunciations of each.
다음은 PART 1 지문 유형 중 자동 응답 메시지에 자주 쓰이는 어휘 및 표현들입니다. 각각의 뜻을 익혀 보세요.

- automated
  자동화된
- inconvenience
  불편
- apologize
  사과하다
- customer service
  고객 서비스
- instruction
  지시
- stay on the line
  전화를 끊지 않고 기다리다
- satisfaction
  만족
- representative
  대표, 대리인
- directly
  바로
- currently
  현재, 지금
- business hours
  영업 시간
- leave a message
  메시지를 남기다
- extension
  내선 번호
- reach
  연락하다
- off-hours
  영업 외 시간
- be connected to
  ~와 연결되다
- momentarily
  곧, 금방

Practice 적용 연습

Read the given passage with a cheerful and tender tone of voice while paying attention to the intonation marks.
억양 기호에 주의하며 주어진 지문을 밝고 상냥한 어조로 읽어 보세요.

> Thank you for calling Dr. Henderson's dental office. ↘ Our clinic is currently closed. ↘ If you're calling to schedule an appointment, ↗ press one. ↘ If you're calling about an existing appointment, ↗ press two. ↘ If this is an emergency, ↗ press zero and leave a message. ↘ One of our staff members will contact you as soon as possible. ↘

MINI TEST

🎧 C4 P1 Mini Test, C4 P1 Model Answer

TOEIC Speaking Question 1 of 11   Volume

Hello, you have reached the top tour provider in town, Prime Tours. We offer vacation packages to many destinations, including trips to lovely beaches, pristine rainforests, and even secluded jungles. In fact, we have over a hundred vacation destinations around the world. Please stay on the line, and a representative will be with you shortly.

PREPARATION TIME	RESPONSE TIME
00:00:45	00:00:45

Translation 해석

안녕하세요. 이 지역 최고의 여행사, Prime Tours입니다. 저희는 아름다운 해변, 자연 그대로의 우림, 심지어 외진 곳에 있는 정글 여행을 포함하는 다양한 여행지로의 휴가 패키지를 제공하고 있습니다. 실제로, 저희는 전 세계 100곳이 넘는 휴양지를 보유하고 있습니다. 잠시 대기해 주시면 곧 담당자와 연결해 드리겠습니다.

TOEIC Speaking Question 2 of 11

Thank you for calling the Hoop-It-Up Basketball Club. No one is available to pick up your call at this time. If you'd like more details about our business hours or location, please press one. For more information on club memberships, private lessons, and coaching staff, please visit our website at any time.

PREPARATION TIME	RESPONSE TIME
00:00:45	00:00:45

Translation 해석

Hoop-It-Up Basketball Club에 전화 주셔서 감사합니다. 현재 상담사가 모두 통화 중입니다. 당사의 영업 시간, 또는 위치에 대한 자세한 정보를 원하시면, 1번을 눌러 주세요. 클럽 회원권, 개인 레슨, 코치진에 대해 자세한 사항을 알고 싶으시다면, 언제든지 저희 웹사이트를 방문해 주세요.

PART 2 Describe a picture

GROUNDWORK

📍 Type Analysis: Park/Tourist Attraction 유형 분석: 공원/관광지

Useful Expression 유용한 표현

These are the vocabulary and expressions that can be used when describing a picture taken from a park or tourist attraction in PART 2. Try to learn the meanings and pronunciations of each.
다음은 PART 2 사진 유형 중 공원이나 관광지에서 찍힌 사진을 묘사할 때 유용하게 쓸 수 있는 어휘 및 표현들입니다. 각각의 뜻을 익혀 보세요.

- **look into the distance** 먼 곳을 보다
- **face each other** 서로 마주 보다
- **tourist attraction** 관광지, 관광 명소
- **bicycle lane** 자전거 도로
- **grassy field** 잔디밭
- **pathway** 좁은 길
- **lush tree** 무성한 나무
- **be gathered together** 모여 있다
- **bush** 덤불
- **sit around** 둘러앉아 있다
- **cross one's legs [arms]** ~의 다리[팔]를 꼬다
- **cathedral** 성당
- **relax** 쉬다
- **clock tower** 시계탑
- **look around** 둘러보다

Sample Practice 예제 연습

Ideation

Look at the picture and think about what you want to focus on when describing it.
다음 사진을 보고, 무엇을 묘사할 것인지 생각해 보세요.

- Where do you think this picture was taken?
- Where are the people sitting?
- What kind of relationship do you think they have?
- What kind of clothes are they wearing?
- Can you guess what season it is by looking at the picture?
- What do you feel when you look at the picture?

Answer Structure

Now, follow the steps below to organize your response systematically.
이제, 아래 단계에 따라 답변을 체계적으로 구성해 보세요.

STEP 1 — Place & Number of people

Begin by stating the location where the picture might have been taken. If possible, also mention the number of people in the picture.

Pattern
This picture was taken _____.
- at a park

STEP 2 — Main person or thing

Describe the main person or thing in the picture.

Pattern 1
The first thing I'm noticing is _____.
- five people sitting around on a grassy field

Pattern 2
By looking at _____, _____.
- clothes they are wearing, I can guess that it's spring

STEP 3 — Surroundings

Say a few things about the rest of the picture by using location descriptions.

Pattern 1
In the background, _____.
- I see some trees and people walking

Pattern 2
Also, _____.
- I think there is a pathway

STEP 4 — Opinions or feelings about the picture

Conclude by expressing your thoughts or feelings about the picture.

Pattern 1
It seems like _____.
- a typical scene from a park

Pattern 2
I like/don't like this picture because _____.
- it looks like people are having a good time together

MINI TEST

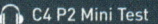

🎧 C4 P2 Mini Test

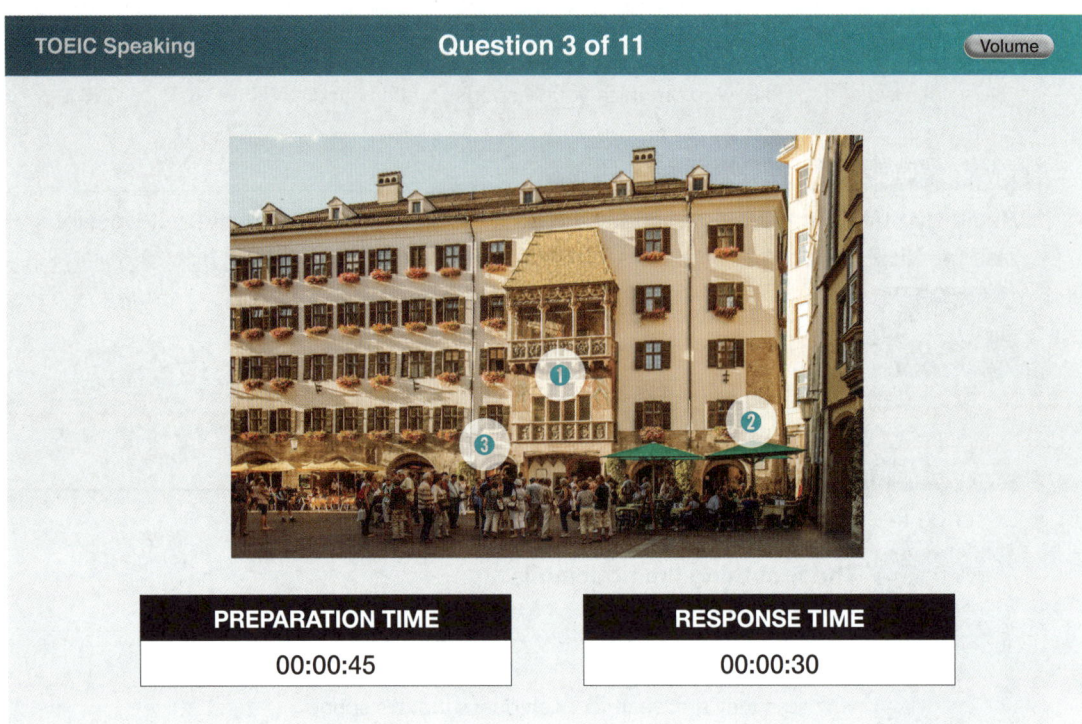

HINT 1 Answer Structure 답변 구조

I think this picture was taken at a tourist attraction somewhere in Europe.

❶ The first thing I notice is _____.

❷ On the right side, _____.

❸ In the middle, _____.

It looks like a pleasant day with a nice atmosphere.

HINT 2 Useful Expression 유용한 표현

- unique architecture
  독특한 건축물
- rectangular
  네모진
- well-maintained
  잘 관리된
- nice atmosphere
  좋은 분위기
- facade
  정면
- group of people
  무리 지어 있는 사람들
- clear sky
  맑은 하늘
- late afternoon
  늦은 오후

TOEIC Speaking   Question 4 of 11   Volume

PREPARATION TIME
00:00:45

RESPONSE TIME
00:00:30

⌈**HINT 1 Answer Structure** 답변 구조

I think this picture was taken at a city park.

❶ **The first thing I notice is** _____ .

❷ **Right behind** _____ , _____ .

❸ **In the background,** _____ .

It seems like two friends are enjoying each other's company.

⌈**HINT 2 Useful Expression** 유용한 표현

- **city park**
  도심 속 공원
- **have small talk**
  잡담을 나누다
- **face each other**
  서로 마주 보다
- **cross one's legs**
  ~의 다리를 꼬다
- **laugh**
  크게 웃다
- **sneakers**
  운동화
- **sleeveless shirt**
  민소매 셔츠
- **braided hair**
  땋은 머리

Chapter 4 PART 2 Describe a picture **117**

Model Answer 모범 답안

C4 P2 Model Answer

3. I think this picture was taken at a tourist attraction somewhere in Europe.

   ❶ **The first thing I notice is** a unique building with rectangular windows. The building seems quite old but well-maintained.

   ❷ **On the right side,** I see a little café. It seems like people are enjoying their time.

   ❸ **In the middle,** I see a group of people. By looking at the clothes they are wearing, I can tell that it's the spring season.

   It looks like a pleasant day with a nice atmosphere.

4. I think this picture was taken at a city park.

   ❶ **The first thing I notice is** two women sitting on a wooden bench. They are facing each other and having small talk. The woman on the left is wearing a blue and black checked shirt, and the woman on the right is wearing a yellow sleeveless shirt.

   ❷ **Right behind** them, there is a grassy field.

   ❸ **In the background,** I see a lot of trees and some buildings.

   It seems like two friends are enjoying each other's company.

Translation 해석

3. 이 사진은 유럽 어딘가의 관광지에서 찍힌 사진인 것 같습니다.

   ❶ **가장 먼저 눈에 띄는 것은** 직사각형 창문들이 있는 독특한 건물입니다. 건물은 꽤 오래되어 보이지만 잘 관리되어 있습니다.

   ❷ **오른쪽에는** 작은 카페가 보입니다. 사람들이 각자의 시간을 즐기고 있는 것 같습니다.

   ❸ **중앙에는** 무리 지어 서 있는 사람들이 보입니다. 그들의 옷차림을 보면 계절이 봄이라는 것을 알 수 있습니다.

   좋은 분위기의 기분 좋은 날인 것처럼 보입니다.

4. 이 사진은 도심 속 공원에서 찍힌 것 같습니다.

   ❶ **가장 먼저 눈에 띄는 것은** 나무 벤치에 앉아 있는 두 명의 여자들입니다. 그들은 마주 보고 잡담을 나누는 중입니다. 왼쪽 여자는 파란색과 검은색의 체크 무늬 셔츠를 입고 있고 오른쪽 여자는 노란색 민소매 셔츠를 입고 있습니다.

   ❷ **그들 바로 뒤에는** 잔디밭이 있습니다.

   ❸ **뒤편에는** 많은 나무들과 몇몇 건물들이 보입니다.

   두 친구 모두 즐거운 시간을 보내고 있는 것처럼 보입니다.

PART 3 Respond to questions

GROUNDWORK

📍 Master The Basics 이론 학습

Background Knowledge 배경 지식

You will learn more patterns that could give you ideas on how to answer the questions in PART 3. Remember, when you answer the questions, all statements do not have to be true.

이번 단원에서는 PART 3에 출제되는 문제에 답변할 때 활용할 만한 소재를 몇 가지 더 학습합니다. 질문에 대답할 때 답변이 반드시 사실일 필요는 없음을 꼭 기억해 두세요.

Routine & Habit

You can talk about your routine or habit to answer the questions using the sentence patterns as follows:

- I am a morning person [an early bird], so ….
- I am a night person [a night owl], so ….

e.g.
Question: How often do you play computer games? And when do you play them?
Answer: I play computer games every day. I play them at night because I'm a night person.

Personality

You can also use the sentence patterns to describe your personality as follows:

- I am an introvert/extrovert, so ….
- I am a bit impatient [quick-tempered], so ….
- I am an easy-going person, so ….
- I consider myself pretty diligent, so ….

e.g.
Question: How many times a week do you go to a gym?
Answer: On average, I go to a gym once a week. I am a bit lazy, so it's hard for me to go to a gym more often than that.

Practice 적용 연습

Based on what you have learned, practice answering the following questions.
학습한 내용을 바탕으로, 다음 질문에 답변해 보세요.

Question

1. **Question**: When did you last visit a museum?
   Answer: I visited a museum _____. That's because _____.

2. **Question**: Do you usually visit museums alone or with someone?
   Answer: I usually visit museums _____. That's because _____.

3. **Question**: Would you rather pay for a guided tour of a museum or explore on your own?
   Answer:
   - **Topic sentence** _____.
   - **Time killer** _____.
   - **Reason 1** Firstly, _____.
   - **Reason 2** In addition, _____.
   - **Wrap up** Therefore, _____.

Model Answer

1. last week in the morning, I'm a morning person
2. with my friends, I am an extrovert who enjoys spending time with others
3.
   - **Topic sentence** I would pay for a guided tour
   - **Time killer** I have a few reasons why
   - **Reason 1** I'm an extrovert, so I find it much more exciting to tour with others
   - **Reason 2** I really enjoy taking my time to explore museums with guided tours because I am quite an easy-going person
   - **Wrap up** I would pay for a guided tour

MINI TEST

C4 P3 Mini Test

TOEIC Speaking   Question 5 of 11   Volume

Imagine that US News is writing a column about college students in your country. You have agreed to participate in a telephone interview about study routines.

When do you usually work on your school assignments, and where do you usually do them?

PREPARATION TIME	RESPONSE TIME
00:00:03	00:00:15

TOEIC Speaking   Question 6 of 11   Volume

Imagine that US News is writing a column about college students in your country. You have agreed to participate in a telephone interview about study routines.

Do you enjoy doing group projects? Why or why not?

PREPARATION TIME	RESPONSE TIME
00:00:03	00:00:15

TOEIC Speaking   Question 7 of 11   Volume

Imagine that US News is writing a column about college students in your country. You have agreed to participate in a telephone interview about study routines.

Do you study more or less than you did a year ago? What makes you think so?

PREPARATION TIME	RESPONSE TIME
00:00:03	00:00:30

Model Answer 모범 답안

C4 P3 Model Answer

5. I usually work on my school assignments in the morning because I'm an early bird, and I usually do them at the school library.

6. Yes, I do enjoy participating in group projects. That's because I am an extrovert, and I love meeting people and collaborating on tasks.

7.
- **Topic sentence** I think I study more now than I did a year ago.
- **Time killer** I have a few reasons why.
- **Reason 1** First of all, as I've grown older, I've become an early bird. I usually wake up at 6 in the morning. Since there isn't much to do right after I wake up, I just study.
- **Reason 2** Also, I try to be a diligent person, so I study whenever I have the time.
- **Wrap up** So, I think I study more now than I did a year ago.

Translation 해석

상황 설정
US News라는 곳에서 여러분이 사는 나라의 대학생에 대해 칼럼을 쓰고 있다고 가정해 봅시다. 여러분은 공부 습관에 관한 유선 설문 조사에 응하기로 했습니다.

5번 질문, 모범 답안
Q: 당신은 학교 과제를 주로 언제, 어디서 하나요?
A: 저는 일찍 일어나기 때문에 보통 아침에 학교 과제를 합니다. 보통은 학교 도서관에서 과제를 합니다.

6번 질문, 모범 답안
Q: 조별 과제 하는 것을 선호하시나요? 왜 그런가요?
A: 네, 저는 조별 과제에 참여하는 걸 좋아합니다. 저는 외향적인 성격이라, 사람들을 만나는 것과 어떤 일을 협력해서 하는 것을 좋아하기 때문입니다.

7번 질문, 모범 답안
Q: 1년 전보다 공부를 더 많이 합니까, 혹은 적게 합니까? 왜 그렇게 생각하나요?
A:
- **Topic sentence** 1년 전보다는 더 많이 공부를 하는 것 같습니다.
- **Time killer** 몇 가지 이유가 있습니다.
- **Reason 1** 우선 나이가 들면서, 아침형 인간이 되었습니다. 저는 보통 아침 6시에 일어나는데요. 일어나자마자 할 만한 일이 별로 없기 때문에, 저는 그냥 공부를 합니다.
- **Reason 2** 또한, 부지런한 사람이 되려고 노력하기 때문에 시간이 날 때마다 공부를 합니다.
- **Wrap up** 그래서 저는 1년 전보다 지금 더 공부를 많이 한다고 생각합니다.

PART 4 Respond to questions using information provided

GROUNDWORK

Type Analysis: Schedule 유형 분석: 일정표

Background Knowledge 배경 지식

In PART 4, you will encounter different types of information materials. We will now look at the interview/personal schedules. Take note of how "you" is used in the answer, which makes it sound more as if you are speaking directly to the caller. Sometimes the items on the schedule will be marked as "canceled" or "postponed", so pay attention to how those are answered as well.

PART 4에서는 다양한 형태의 자료로 정보가 제시됩니다. 이번 단원에서는 면접 혹은 개인 일정표 유형을 살펴볼 예정입니다. 특히, 문의자와 직접 대화하고 있다는 느낌을 주기 위해 "you"를 어떻게 사용하면 되는지, 취소되거나 연기된 일정에 대해서는 어떻게 정보를 전달하면 되는지 주의 깊게 살펴보세요.

How to use "you" in the answer

Richmond Broadcasting Networks Inc.
Job interview schedule
Aug. 23, 9:00 a.m. ~ 5:00 p.m.
Interview Location: Conference Room A

Time	Name of Applicant	Position	Note
9:00 a.m.	Kevin Perkins	Data Journalist	Master's degree in Journalism
10:00 a.m.	Sarah Chung	Hair and Makeup artist	5 years of experience
11:00 a.m.	John McAllister	Control room technician	2 years of experience
1:00 p.m.	Lloyd Singh	Custodian	Phone interview
3:00 p.m.	Linda Hall	Television studio technician	4 years of experience
5:00 p.m.	Justin Thomas	Media operator	12 years of experience

Narration: Hello, I'm interviewing some job applicants tomorrow, but I think I lost the copy of the interview schedule. So, I'd like to get some information.

8. **Question:** When does the first interview begin, and who am I interviewing?
   Answer: The first interview will begin at 9 a.m., and *you* are interviewing Kevin Perkins.

9. **Question:** We are mostly looking to hire people with a lot of experience. We don't have any applicants with more than 10 years of experience, do we?
   Answer: I am afraid that *you* have the wrong information. We do have one applicant with 12 years of experience. His name is Justin Thomas.

10. Question: We are in desperate need of some skilled technicians right now. Can you give me all the details about the interviews for the technician position?

Answer: Sure. There are two interviews scheduled for the technician position. First, **you** will have an interview with John McAllister for the control room technician position at 11 a.m. He has 2 years of experience. Also, **you** will interview Linda Hall for a television studio technician position at 3 p.m. She has 4 years of experience.

How to inform canceled or postponed schedule

Henry Blackwood, Zoologist
Schedule for Monday, Aug. 23

8:00 ~ 9:15 a.m.	Give lecture (Native mammal types)
9:15 ~ 10:00 a.m.	Video conference call (Supervisor of Orinda Research Station)
10:00 a.m. ~ Noon	Update research (Mammal ecosystem study)
Noon ~ 1:00 p.m.	Lunch
1:00 ~ 3:00 p.m.	Visit (Taronga Zoo)
3:00 ~ 4:30 p.m.	Work on Orinda research report
4:30 ~ 5:30 p.m.	~~Meeting (Jennifer Han, biologist from Irvine lab)~~ Postponed to Aug. 30 at 4 p.m.

Question: I'm pretty sure I have a meeting with Jennifer Han, the biologist from Irvine Lab. The meeting is scheduled for 4:30 p.m., right?

Answer: Actually, you have the wrong information. The meeting with Jennifer Han **is postponed to August 13th at 4 p.m.**

MINI TEST

 C4 P4 Mini Test

TOEIC Speaking Question 8-10 of 11 Volume

J.R. Language Institute - Interviews for instructors June 5, 9:00 a.m. ~ 5:00 p.m. / Meeting Room G			
Time	Applicant Name	Class	Previous Employer
9:00 a.m.	Deborah Sanford	English Grammar	Brilliant Institute
11:00 a.m.	Patty Wang	Basic Chinese	Macker's Institute
~~1:00 p.m.~~	~~Jenny Lopez~~	~~Basic Spanish~~	~~Sound Institute~~ Canceled
3:00 p.m.	Kyle Mitchell	Advanced English Grammar	Brilliant Institute
4:00 p.m.	Patrick Tang	Advanced Chinese	Bei Long Institute

PREPARATION TIME
00:00:45

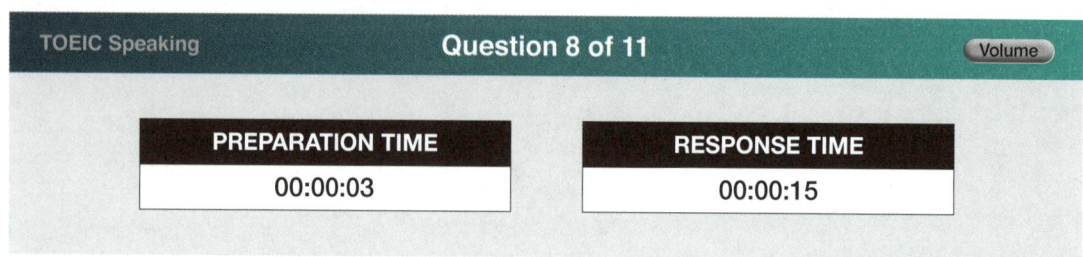

HINT Useful Expression 유용한 표현

- interview 면접
- start at ~에 시작하다
- be held in ~에서 진행되다

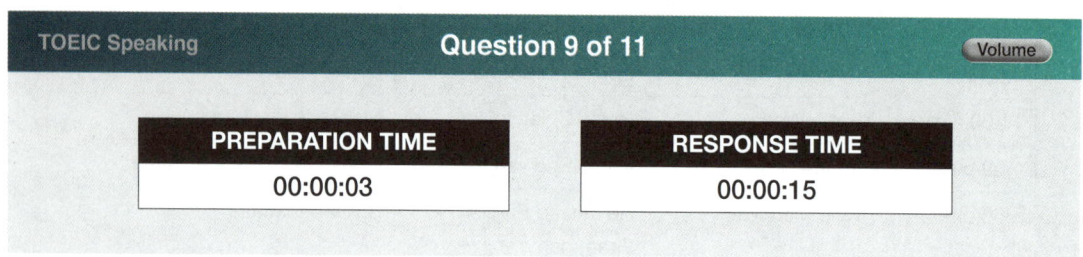

HINT Useful Expression 유용한 표현

- previous 이전의
- institute 학원, 기관
- instructor 강사
- be canceled 취소되다
- applicant 지원자

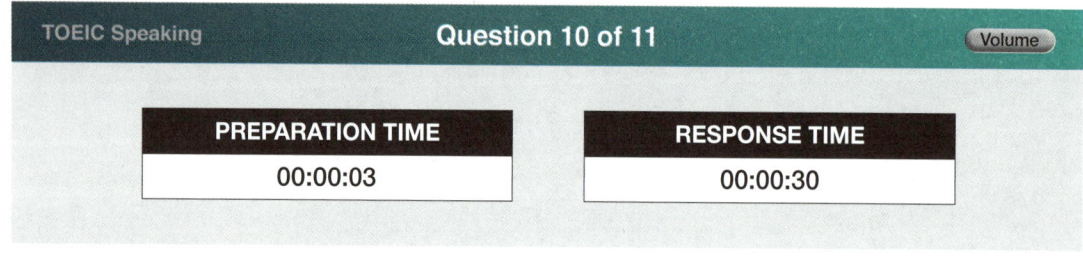

HINT Useful Expression 유용한 표현

- hire 고용하다
- advanced 상급의
- apply for ~에 지원하다
- position 직무

Model Answer 모범 답안

🎧 C4 P4 Model Answer

J.R. Language Institute - Interviews for instructors
June 5, 9:00 a.m. ~ 5:00 p.m. / ❽ Meeting Room G

Time	Applicant Name	Class	Previous Employer
❽ 9:00 a.m.	Deborah Sanford	English Grammar	Brilliant Institute
❿ 11:00 a.m.	Patty Wang	Basic Chinese	Macker's Institute
❾ 1:00 p.m.	~~Jenny Lopez~~	~~Basic Spanish~~	~~Sound Institute~~ Canceled
3:00 p.m.	Kyle Mitchell	Advanced English Grammar	Brilliant Institute
❿ 4:00 p.m.	Patrick Tang	Advanced Chinese	Bei Long Institute

Narration: Hi, I'm interviewing applicants for our new instructors tomorrow. But I forgot to bring my schedule from the office, and I was hoping you could check some information for me.

8. Question: What time is the first interview, and where will the interviews be held?
   Answer: The first interview will start at 9 a.m., and the interviews will be held in Meeting Room G.

9. Question: In the previous years, we've had some great instructors from the Sound Institute. We have an interview with an applicant from the Sound Institute tomorrow, right?
   Answer: I am afraid that you have the wrong information. The interview with an applicant from the Sound Institute has been canceled.

10. Question: I'm really interested in hiring instructors for Chinese classes. Could you give me all the details about the interviews with applicants applying for instructor positions for the Chinese classes?
   Answer: Sure. There are two applicants applying for Chinese classes. First, there will be an interview with Patty Wang for Basic Chinese at 11 a.m. She's from the Macker's Institute. Also, you will interview Patrick Tang for Advanced Chinese at 4 p.m. He's from the Bei Long Institute.

Translation 해석

나레이션
안녕하세요. 내일 신규 강사 지원자들 면접 볼 예정인데요. 깜빡하고 일정표를 사무실에 두고 왔습니다. 몇 가지 정보를 확인해 주실 수 있나요?

8번 질문, 모범 답안
Q: 첫 번째 면접은 언제, 어디서 진행되나요?
A: 첫 번째 면접은 오전 9시, G 회의실에서 진행됩니다.

9번 질문, 모범 답안
Q: 지난 몇 년 간 Sound Institute 출신의 강사분들이 훌륭하셨는데요. 내일 Sound Institute 출신 강사분과의 면접이 있죠?
A: 유감스럽게도 잘못 알고 계십니다. Sound Institute 출신 지원자와의 면접은 취소되었습니다.

10번 질문, 모범 답안
Q: 중국어 강사를 고용하는 데 특히 관심이 많습니다. 중국어 강사로 지원하는 분들과의 면접 일정에 대해 자세히 알려주시겠습니까?
A: 물론입니다. 중국어 강사로 두 분이 지원하셨는데요. 먼저 오전 11시에 기초 중국어 수업의 Patty Wang님과 면접이 있습니다. Macker's 학원 출신이시네요. 그리고 오후 4시에는 상급 중국어 수업의 Patrick Tang님과 면접이 예정되어 있습니다. 그분은 Bei Long 학원 출신이세요.

PART 5 Express an opinion

GROUNDWORK

📍 Master The Basics 이론 학습

Background Knowledge 배경 지식

In PART 5, you'll frequently encounter topics related to technology and online services. To answer the questions, practice utilizing "the Internet" as a topic in your answer.

PART 5에서는 기술 및 온라인 관련 주제가 자주 출제됩니다. 따라서, '인터넷'을 소재로 답변을 풀어 나가는 연습을 해두면 실전에서 큰 도움을 받을 수 있습니다.

Useful Idea Pattern : I-pattern

The "I" stands for "the Internet". This pattern will not only answer questions about the Internet, but also about a variety of other topics. Take a look at the examples of the following "I-pattern" and see how these examples are applied.

Idea Pattern Examples

- I think it's because of the Internet.
  저는 그것이 인터넷 때문이라고 생각합니다.

- I think _____ because it's based on the Internet.
  저는 그것이 인터넷을 기반으로 하기 때문에 _____ 라고 생각합니다.

- Nowadays, we can easily access the Internet by using computers or smartphones.
  요즘, 우리는 컴퓨터나 스마트폰으로 인터넷에 쉽게 접속할 수 있습니다.

- This implies that it is convenient to _____ anywhere at any time.
  그것은 언제 어디에서나 편리하게 _____ 이 가능하다는 것을 의미합니다.

- Besides, there is literally nothing that we cannot do with the Internet.
  게다가, 말 그대로 우리가 인터넷으로 못 하는 일은 없습니다.

- In many cases, I believe our society is run by computer and Internet technology.
  다방면에서, 우리 사회는 컴퓨터와 인터넷 기술에 기반을 두어 운영된다고 생각합니다.

How to Apply

Question:

Do you agree or disagree with the following statement?

People today have a better life than people in the past.

Give specific reasons or examples to support your opinion.

Answer:
I agree that people today have a better life than people in the past. I think it's because of the Internet. The Internet has become so useful and convenient for people. It saves us time, money, and energy. I believe the Internet can be a useful tool in any situation. Nowadays, we can easily access the Internet by using computers or smartphones. This implies you can communicate with people and access information from all over the world at any time and from anywhere. Additionally, there is nothing we cannot do with the Internet. You can work remotely, use food delivery services, and shop without having to move. Therefore, I agree that people today have a better life than people in the past.

Practice 적용 연습

Based on what you have learned, answer the following questions.
학습한 내용을 바탕으로, 다음 질문에 답변해 보세요.

Question
Do you agree or disagree with the following statement?
Communicating face-to-face is better than any other way of communicating.
Give specific reasons or examples to support your opinion.

Apply the Idea Pattern
I disagree that communicating face-to-face is better than any other way of communicating. I think online communication is the best way to communicate. I think online communication is very convenient because it's **1.** _____.
Nowadays, **2.** _____. That means you can **3.** _____ at any time and from anywhere. Besides, I believe our society. **4.** _____, which makes online communication much easier. Therefore, I disagree that communicating face-to-face is better than any other way of communicating.

Model Answer
1. based on the Internet
2. we can easily access the Internet by using computers or smartphones
3. communicate with people
4. is run by computers and Internet technology

MINI TEST

C4 P5 Mini Test

TOEIC Speaking Question 11 of 11 Volume

What invention do you think has impacted our society the most?
Choose ONE of the options below and give specific reasons or examples to support your answer.
- Electricity
- Automobile
- Computer

PREPARATION TIME	RESPONSE TIME
00:00:45	00:00:60

Model Answer 모범 답안

🎧 C4 P5 Model Answer

I think computers have impacted our society the most. This is because computers have made it possible for us to use the Internet. The Internet has changed our lives and, furthermore, transformed industries and society. **There is literally nothing we cannot do with the Internet. The Internet makes it incredibly convenient to access information, get what you need, and communicate with people anywhere at any time.** As more and more people incorporate the Internet as an essential tool in their lives, industries and society have also adapted accordingly. Nowadays, **I believe our society is run by computers and Internet technology**. Therefore, I think computers have impacted our society the most.

Translation 해석

문제
어떤 발명이 우리 사회의 가장 큰 영향을 미쳤다고 생각합니까?
아래의 보기 중 하나를 골라 구체적인 근거와 사례를 들어 의견을 뒷받침하십시오.

- 전기
- 자동차
- 컴퓨터

모범 답안
저는 컴퓨터가 우리 사회에 가장 큰 영향을 미쳤다고 생각합니다. 그렇게 생각하는 이유는 컴퓨터를 통해 우리가 인터넷을 사용할 수 있게 되었기 때문입니다. 인터넷은 우리의 삶을 바꾸어 놓았고, 나아가 산업과 사회를 변화시켰습니다. **말 그대로, 인터넷을 통해 우리가 할 수 없는 것은 없습니다. 인터넷은 언제 어디서든 정보에 접근하고, 필요한 것을 얻고, 사람들과 소통하는 것을 매우 편리하게 만듭니다.** 점점 더 많은 사람들이 인터넷을 삶의 필수적인 도구로 채택함에 따라 산업과 사회도 이에 맞게 변화했습니다. 요즘에는 **우리 사회가 컴퓨터와 인터넷 기술에 의해 돌아가고 있다고 생각합니다**. 그러므로 저는 컴퓨터가 우리 사회에 가장 큰 영향을 미쳤다고 생각합니다.

REVIEW TEST 4

TOEIC Speaking Question 1 of 11 Volume

You have reached the Mackin's Computer Academy. We offer classes in software design, network administration, and computer repair. Unfortunately, our offices are currently closed. To speak with a staff member, please call back between ten a.m. and six p.m. on any weekday. For detailed information regarding course content and schedule, please visit our website!

PREPARATION TIME	RESPONSE TIME
00:00:45	00:00:45

TOEIC Speaking Question 2 of 11 Volume

You have reached Big Seven Sporting Goods. Unfortunately, no one is available to take your call at this time. For information about our hours, location, and special discounts, please visit our website. If you would like to communicate with a store associate, please press "one" and leave a brief message. An available associate will contact you shortly.

PREPARATION TIME	RESPONSE TIME
00:00:45	00:00:45

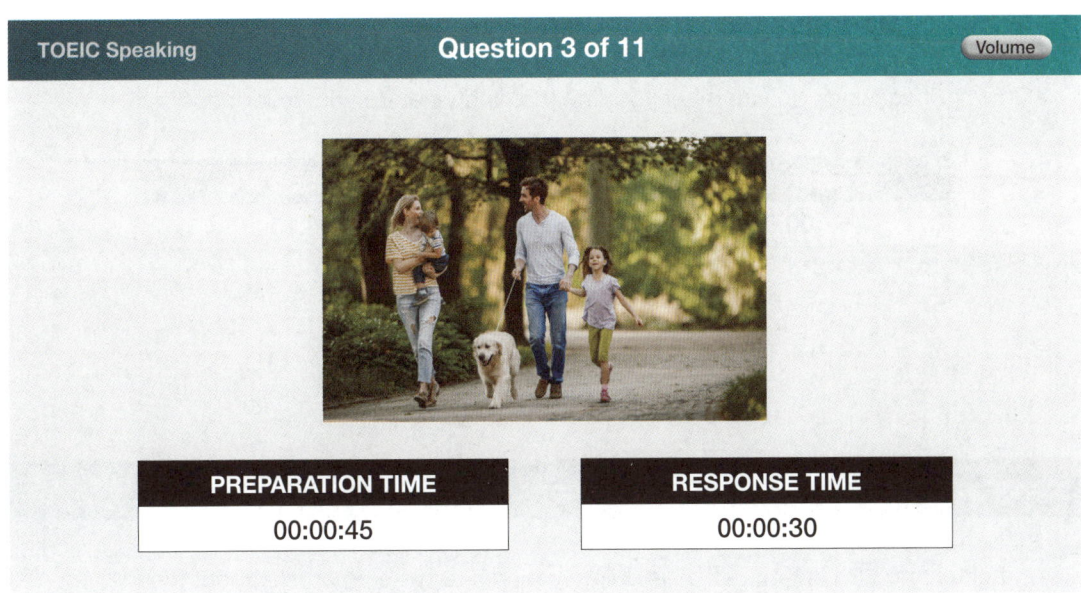

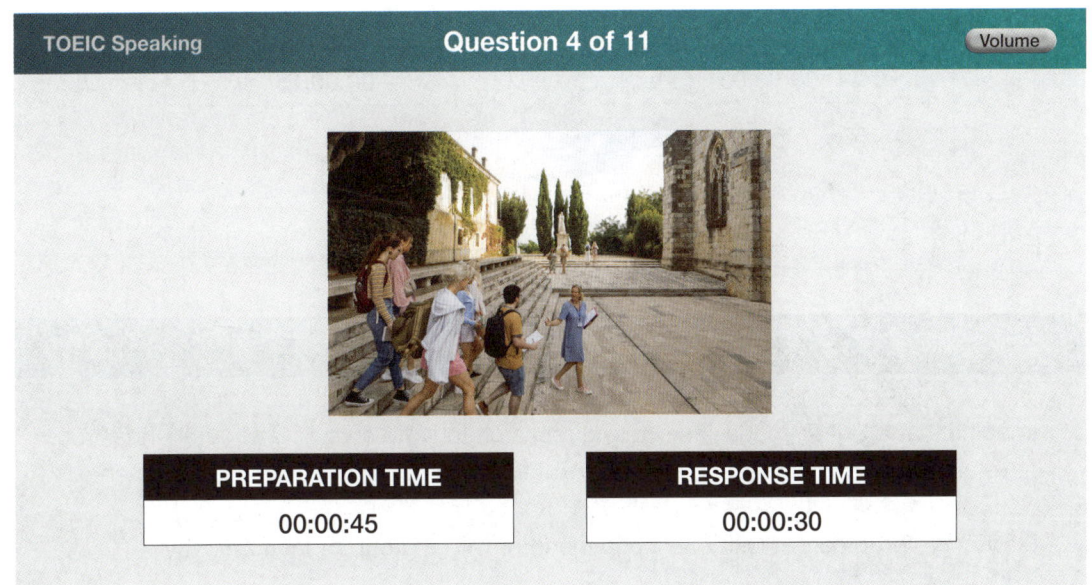

| TOEIC Speaking | Question 5 of 11 | |

Imagine that a British magazine is doing research to write an article about friends. You have agreed to participate in a telephone interview about doing activities with friends.

On what occasions do you meet your friends, and what do you usually do?

PREPARATION TIME	RESPONSE TIME
00:00:03	00:00:15

| TOEIC Speaking | Question 6 of 11 | |

Imagine that a British magazine is doing research to write an article about friends. You have agreed to participate in a telephone interview about doing activities with friends.

Do you hang out with your friends more or less than you used to? Why?

PREPARATION TIME	RESPONSE TIME
00:00:03	00:00:15

| TOEIC Speaking | Question 7 of 11 | |

Imagine that a British magazine is doing research to write an article about friends. You have agreed to participate in a telephone interview about doing activities with friends.

Do you prefer to go out with one close friend or with a group of friends? Why?

PREPARATION TIME	RESPONSE TIME
00:00:03	00:00:30

TOEIC Speaking

Question 8-10 of 11

Saferoad Groceries
Interview schedule
Fri, Sep. 11
Staff Lounge

Time	Applicant	Position	Current Employer
11:00 ~ 11:30 a.m.	Emily Jenkins	Cashier	EZ Office Supplies
11:30 a.m. ~ Noon	Irene Brown	Deli manager	Chop Restaurant
1:00 ~ 1:30 p.m.	Terry Houston	Assistant store manager	Joe's Apparel
1:30 ~ 2:00 p.m.	Douglas Cage	Butcher	Charlie's Steakhouse
2:00 ~ 2:30 p.m.	Marry Kim	Custodian	See-U Supermarket
2:30 ~ 3:00 p.m.	Jose Macias	Deli manager	Tubeway Sandwich

PREPARATION TIME
00:00:45

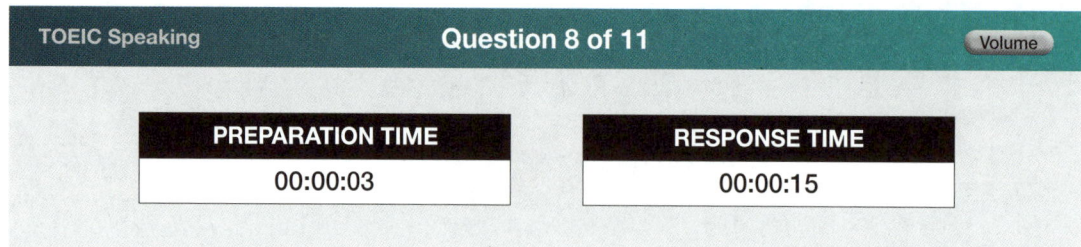

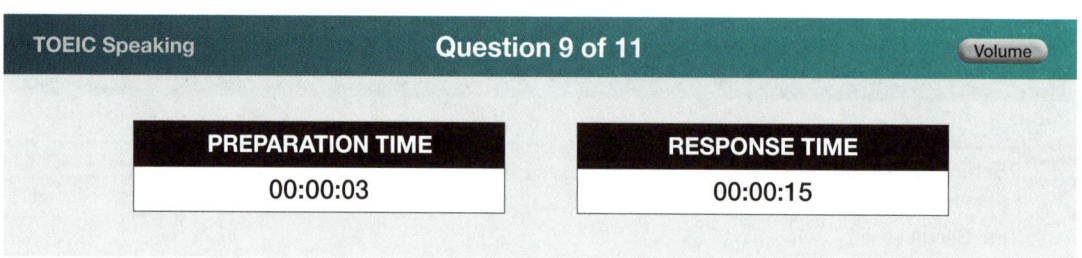

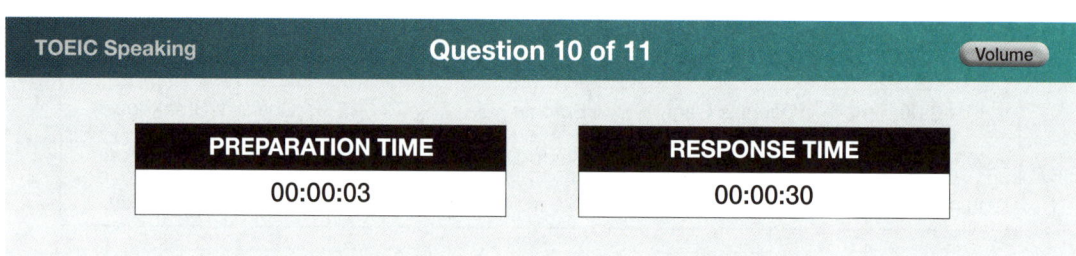

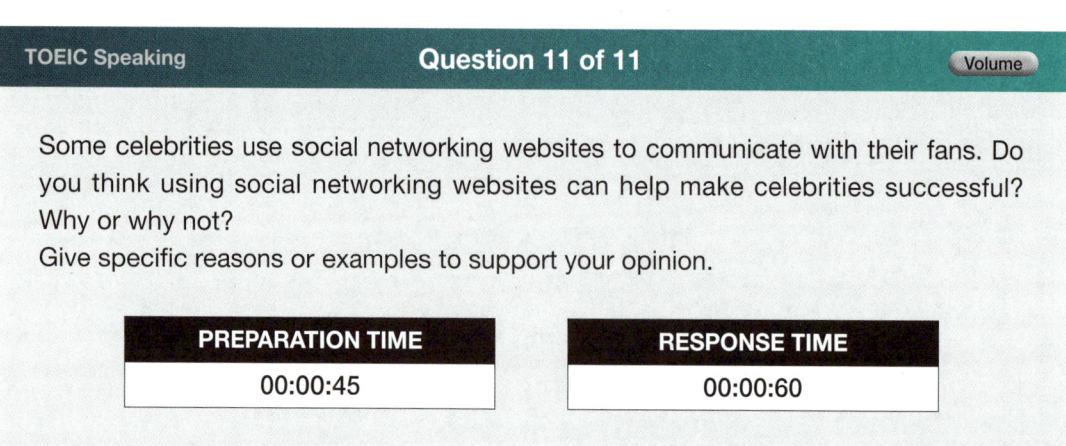

Some celebrities use social networking websites to communicate with their fans. Do you think using social networking websites can help make celebrities successful? Why or why not?
Give specific reasons or examples to support your opinion.

Chapter 5

PART 1
Read a text aloud

PART 2
Describe a picture

PART 3
Respond to questions

PART 4
Respond to questions using information provided

PART 5
Express an opinion

REVIEW TEST 5

PART 1 Read a text aloud

GROUNDWORK

📍 Master The Basics 이론 학습

Background Knowledge 배경 지식

Read the explanations and learn the pause rules in English.
다음 설명을 읽고 영어의 끊어 읽기 규칙을 익혀 보세요.

- Using pauses effectively when reading a text will make the audience understand your speech better.
- Look at the following cases and try to analyze where to pause when you read a text.

The Comma Pause

Give short pauses whenever a comma is used in the text.

e.g. For dinner, v the chef is planning to prepare barbecue chicken, v beef stews, v and a variety of side dishes.

The Conjunction Pause

Give short pauses whenever a conjunction would be used in the text. Use pauses in front of the conjunction.

e.g.
- My dad bought a new TV v and a coffee table.
- Do you prefer beef v or chicken?
- My girlfriend likes flowers, v but she likes money more.
- He screamed v because he had hurt his arm.

The Relative Pronoun Pause

Give short pauses whenever relative pronouns are used in the text. Pause right before the relative pronoun.

e.g.
- The person v who sent the money was my grandfather.
- The man v who we talked about is the president of the company.
- This is the guy v whose car was stolen last week.
- My friend bought a house in San Francisco, v which is his favorite city.

Type Analysis: Introduction 유형 분석: 소개 연설

- Introduction is a text that a media host or event host uses to introduce invited guests.
- To make the reading sound more natural, use appropriate pauses and focus on linking sounds.
- Make sure the tone of your voice is cheerful and welcoming.

Useful Expressions 유용한 표현

These are the vocabulary and expressions commonly found in the introduction type texts of PART 1. Try to learn the meanings and pronunciations of each.
다음은 PART 1 지문 유형 중 소개 멘트에 자주 쓰이는 어휘 및 표현들입니다. 각각의 뜻을 익혀 보세요.

- introduce
  소개하다
- guest speaker
  초청 연사
- world-renowned
  세계적으로 유명한
- chief executive officer
  최고 경영자
- top-rated
  최고 순위의
- honor
  영광
- looking forward to
  ~을 기대하다
- experience
  경험
- celebrate
  축하하다
- involved
  관여하는
- present
  소개하다, 발표하다
- certainly
  틀림없이
- improve
  개선하다
- support
  지지하다
- momentarily
  곧, 금방
- reach
  연락하다

Practice 적용 연습

Read the given passage with a cheerful and welcoming tone of voice while paying attention to the pause marks.
끊어 읽기 기호에 주의하며 주어진 지문을 밝고 환영하는 듯한 어조로 읽어 보세요.

> It is my honor to introduce v Dr. Hovland v as the new chief of operations. v Dr. Hovland comes to us v from First Children's Hospital v where he spent twenty years v on the operations team. v Needless to say, v we are looking forward to the knowledge, v expertise, v and experience v that he will bring to our institution. v Now, v let's welcome v Dr. Hovland v to the stage!

MINI TEST

🎧 C5 P1 Mini Test, C5 P1 Model Answer

TOEIC Speaking Question 1 of 11 Volume

I want to thank everyone for joining our conference today. It is such an honor to introduce Joseph Kite, our company's new director. With his forty years of business experience all around the world, we are delighted to have him on our side. Mr. Kite will focus on product improvement, marketing, and global network building. Now, let's hear a few words from the man himself, Joseph Kite.

PREPARATION TIME	RESPONSE TIME
00:00:45	00:00:45

Translation 해석

오늘 회의에 참석해 주신 모든 분들께 감사드립니다. 우리 회사 신임 이사인 Joseph Kite 씨를 소개하게 되어 매우 영광입니다. 40년 동안 전 세계에서 비즈니스 경험을 쌓은 그를 우리 회사에 모시게 되어 매우 기쁩니다. Kite 씨는 제품 개선, 마케팅, 그리고 글로벌 네트워크 구축을 담당하실 예정입니다. 이제, Joseph Kite 씨의 말씀을 들어보겠습니다.

TOEIC Speaking Question 2 of 11   Volume

On May 13th, Jazz Radio Z will welcome the legendary jazz artist Kenny Park to the studio in Walnut Creek. Park will be touring and holding concerts in several different cities in May and June. Also, his newest album, which is available online starting next week, features some of his first new tracks in more than five years.

PREPARATION TIME	RESPONSE TIME
00:00:45	00:00:45

Translation 해석

5월 13일, Jazz Radio Z는 Walnut Creek의 스튜디오에서 전설적인 재즈 아티스트 Kenny Park 씨를 모실 예정입니다. Park 씨는 5월과 6월에 여러 도시들에서 콘서트를 여실 예정입니다. 또한, 다음 주 온라인으로 발매될 그의 최신 앨범에는 5년 이상 기다려 온 그의 새로운 트랙이 포함되어 있습니다.

PART 2 Describe a picture

GROUNDWORK

📍 Type Analysis: Station / Airport / Vacation Spot 유형 분석: 역/공항/휴양지

Useful Expression 유용한 표현

These are the vocabulary and expressions that can be used when describing a picture taken at a station, an airport, and a vacation spot in PART 2. Try to learn the meanings and pronunciations of each.
다음은 PART 2 사진 유형 중 역, 공항, 휴양지에서 찍힌 사진을 묘사할 때 유용하게 쓸 수 있는 어휘 및 표현들입니다. 각각의 뜻을 익혀 보세요.

- **platform** 플랫폼
- **book a flight** 항공편을 예약하다
- **train track** 선로
- **destination** 목적지
- **hand luggage** 기내 반입용 수하물
- **business traveler** 출장객
- **boarding gate** 탑승구
- **commute** 통근하다
- **baggage claim** 수하물 찾는 곳
- **approach the station** 역에 들어오다
- **conveyor belt** (물건을 이동시키는) 컨베이어 벨트
- **lie down** 눕다
- **ticket machine** 매표기
- **land** 착륙하다
- **deck chair** 접이식 의자

Sample Practice 예제 연습

Ideation

Look at the picture and think about what you want to focus on when describing it.
다음 사진을 보고, 무엇을 묘사할 것인지 생각해 보세요.

- Where do you think this picture was taken?
- What is the first thing you see?
- What time of the day do you think this picture was taken? Why do you think so?
- What do you think the people are doing?
- Can you guess the season and weather by looking at the picture?
- What do you feel when you look at the picture?

Answer Structure

Now, follow the steps below to organize your response systematically.
이제, 아래 단계에 따라 답변을 체계적으로 구성해 보세요.

STEP 1 Place & Number of people

Begin by stating the location where the picture might have been taken. If possible, also mention the number of people in the picture.

| Pattern 1 | **This picture was taken _____.**
• at a subway station • on a train platform |

| Pattern 2 | **I see _____ people in this picture.**
• many • several |

STEP 2 Main person or thing

Describe the main person or thing in the picture.

| Pattern | **The first thing I notice is _____.**
• a yellow train approaching the station |

STEP 3 Surroundings

Say a few things about the rest of the picture by using location descriptions.

| Pattern 1 | **In the middle, _____.**
• there are two train tracks |

| Pattern 2 | **Also, _____.**
• there is a platform on either side of the train tracks |

STEP 4 Opinions or feelings about the picture

Conclude by expressing your thoughts or feelings about the picture.

| Pattern 1 | **It seems like _____.**
• a typical scene from a train station |

| Pattern 2 | **I like/don't like this picture because _____.**
• it reminds me of my last weekend trip |

MINI TEST

C5 P2 Mini Test

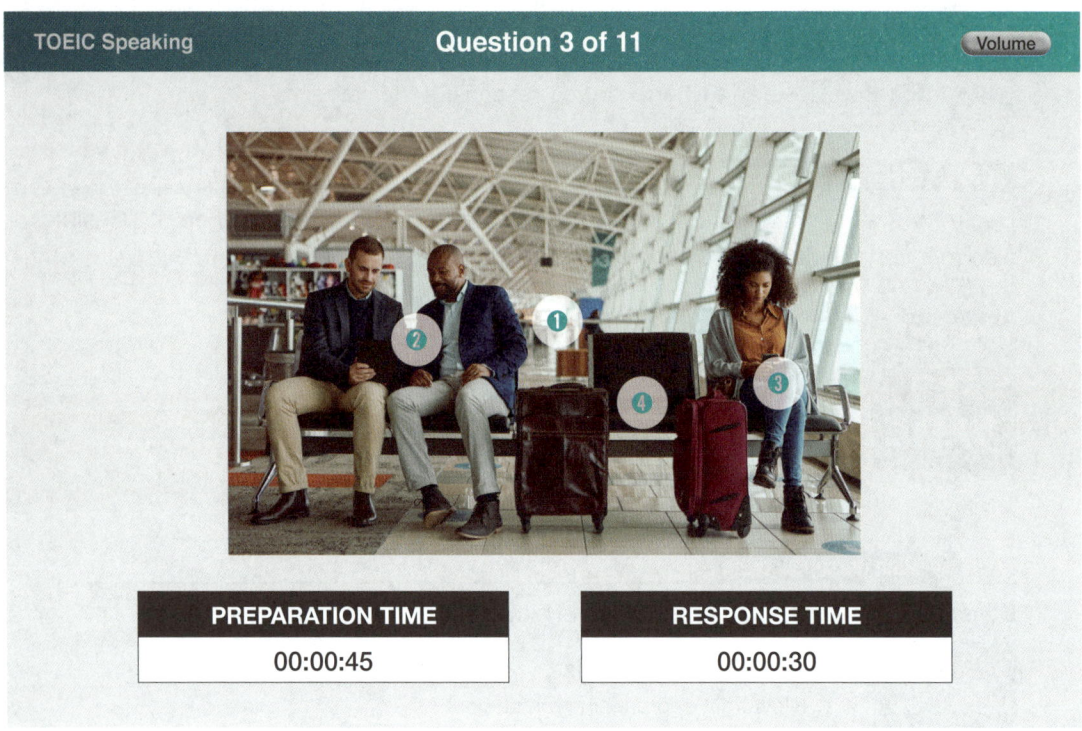

HINT 1 Answer Structure 답변 구조

I think this picture was taken in a waiting area at a terminal.

❶ The first thing I notice is _____ .

❷ On the left side of the picture, _____ .

❸ On the right, _____ .

❹ In between, _____ .

It seems like people are killing time in a waiting area.

HINT 2 Useful Expression 유용한 표현

- terminal
  터미널, 종점, 종착역
- waiting area
  대합실, 대기 공간
- business trip
  출장
- discuss
  의논하다
- exchange information
  정보를 공유하다
- suitcase
  캐리어
- unoccupied seat
  빈자리
- curly hair
  곱슬 머리
- daytime
  낮
- gift shop
  기념품 가게
- kill time
  시간을 때우다
- talk to each other
  대화를 나누다

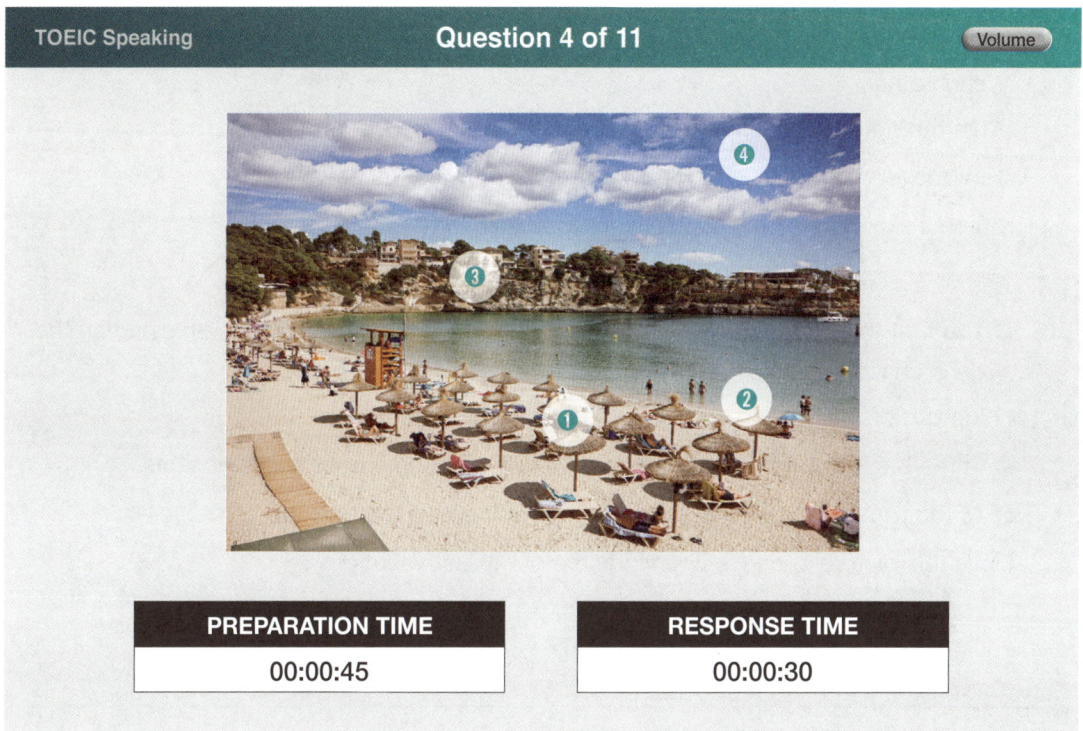

HINT 1 Answer Structure 답변 구조

This picture was taken at a beautiful beach.

❶ The first thing I notice is _____.

❷ In front of _____, _____.

❸ In the background, _____.

❹ At the top of the picture, _____.

I love this picture because it reminds me of my last vacation.

HINT 2 Useful Expression 유용한 표현

- beach
  해변
- lie on
  ~에 누워 있다
- deck chair
  접이식 의자
- rest
  쉬다
- swim
  수영하다
- rocky cliff
  바위 절벽
- lifeguard tower
  구조대가 있는 곳
- enjoy the sun
  햇살을 즐기다

Model Answer 모범 답안 🎧 C5 P2 Model Answer

3. I think this picture was taken in a waiting area at a terminal.
   ❶ **The first thing I notice is** three people sitting on a four-seater bench.
   ❷ **On the left side of the picture,** two men are exchanging information and talking to each other.
   ❸ **On the right,** one woman with curly hair is using a smartphone.
   ❹ **In between,** there is an unoccupied seat and two suitcases.
   It seems like people are killing time in a waiting area.

4. This picture was taken at a beautiful beach.
   ❶ **The first thing I notice is** many parasols. Under them, most people are lying on the deck chairs and enjoying their time.
   ❷ **In front of** them, I can see some people in the water as well.
   ❸ **In the background,** there is a beautiful cliff with some trees and mansions.
   ❹ **At the top of the picture,** there are many clouds in the blue sky.
   I love this picture because it reminds me of my last vacation.

Translation 해석

3. 이 사진은 한 터미널의 대합실에서 찍힌 것 같습니다.
   ❶ **가장 먼저 눈에 띄는 것은** 4인용 벤치에 앉아 있는 세 사람입니다.
   ❷ **사진 왼쪽에는** 두 남자가 정보를 공유하며 이야기를 나누고 있습니다.
   ❸ **오른쪽에는** 곱슬머리의 한 여성이 스마트폰을 사용하고 있습니다.
   ❹ **그 사이에는** 비어 있는 의자와 두 개의 캐리어가 있습니다.
   사람들이 비행기를 기다리며 시간을 때우고 있는 장면처럼 보입니다.

4. 이 사진은 아름다운 해변에서 찍힌 사진입니다.
   ❶ **가장 먼저 눈에 띄는 것은** 수많은 파라솔입니다. 그 아래에는 대부분의 사람들이 접이식 의자에 누워 즐거운 시간을 보내고 있습니다.
   ❷ **그들 앞에는** 바닷물에 들어가 있는 사람들도 몇몇 보입니다.
   ❸ **배경에는** 나무와 저택들이 있는 아름다운 절벽이 있습니다.
   ❹ **사진의 맨 위쪽에는** 푸른 하늘에 구름이 많이 떠 있습니다.
   이 사진이 좋은 이유는 제 지난 휴가를 떠오르게 하기 때문입니다.

PART 3 Respond to questions

GROUNDWORK

📍 Master The Basics 이론 학습

Background Knowledge 배경 지식

Question 7 in PART 3 can be tricky to answer because of the length of the response time. Try to practice including your experience in the answer. This is another good way to lengthen your answer.

PART 3의 7번 문제는 답변 시간이 (5, 6번에 비해) 길기 때문에 답변하기 까다로울 수 있습니다. 이때, 답변에 본인의 경험을 포함해 보세요. 이는 답변 길이를 늘림에 있어 좋은 전략이 되어 줄 것입니다.

Experience

When talking about your experience, try to make the best use of the following expressions:

- In my case, I usually/normally/typically ….
- When I was young, ….
- I have heard that ….
- From my experience, ….
- Since I work a full time job, ….

e.g.

Question: How often do you use food delivery services, and what kind of food do you usually order?
Answer: I use a food delivery service once a week and I usually order Chinese food. **Since I work a full time job,** I don't have much time to cook for myself.

Question: What's the best time of the day to order delivery food?
Answer: The best time of the day to order delivery food is at 3 p.m. **From my experience,** most of the restaurants give out discount coupons at that time.

Question: What resources do you usually use to find options for food delivery in your area?
Answer:
- **Topic sentence** — Well, **in my case,** I like to use food delivery apps.
- **Time killer** — There are several reasons why.
- **Reason 1** — First of all, using the apps can save me time when looking for places that deliver food.
- **Reason 2** — Also, **from my experience,** it helps me make more cost-effective choices by comparing delivery fees.
- **Wrap up** — So, I use food delivery apps when I want to order food for delivery.

Practice 적용 연습

Based on what you have learned, practice answering the following questions.
학습한 내용을 바탕으로, 다음 질문에 답변해 보세요.

Question

1. **Question:** Do you visit bookstores often? Why or why not?
   Answer: _____, I visit bookstores _____. That's because _____.

2. **Question:** How far do you normally travel to go to a bookstore?
   Answer: I usually travel _____ to go to a bookstore. _____.

3. **Question:** If a used bookstore opened in your area, would you visit often?
   Answer:
   - **Topic sentence** _____, _____.
   - **Time killer** _____.
   - **Reason 1** Firstly, _____.
   - **Reason 2** Also, _____.
   - **Wrap up** Therefore, _____.

Model Answer

1. Yes, often, my school major is Literature, so I have to read a lot
2. ten minutes by bus, Because I have heard that it is quite difficult to find when you go there on foot
3.
   - **Topic sentence** Yes, I would visit it often
   - **Time killer** I have a few reasons why
   - **Reason 1** I like buying used books because it reminds me of a good memory. When I was young, I used to go to a used bookstore with my family and had a great time there
   - **Reason 2** from my experience, used books are much cheaper than the new ones
   - **Wrap up** I would visit it often

MINI TEST

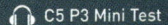

C5 P3 Mini Test

TOEIC Speaking — Question 5 of 11 — Volume

Imagine that an Australian technology magazine is doing research in your country. You have agreed to participate in a telephone interview about smartphone apps.

When was the last time you used a smartphone app, and what kind of app was it?

PREPARATION TIME	RESPONSE TIME
00:00:03	00:00:15

TOEIC Speaking — Question 6 of 11 — Volume

Imagine that an Australian technology magazine is doing research in your country. You have agreed to participate in a telephone interview about smartphone apps.

Do you usually purchase apps for learning or entertainment purposes? Why?

PREPARATION TIME	RESPONSE TIME
00:00:03	00:00:15

TOEIC Speaking — Question 7 of 11 — Volume

Imagine that an Australian technology magazine is doing research in your country. You have agreed to participate in a telephone interview about smartphone apps.

Which of the following factors do you think is the most important when purchasing a smartphone app? Why?

- Price
- User-friendly design
- High-quality customer support

PREPARATION TIME	RESPONSE TIME
00:00:03	00:00:30

Model Answer 모범 답안

🎧 C5 P3 Model Answer

5. The last time I used a smartphone app was a few hours ago, and it was a social media app.

6. I usually purchase apps for learning purposes. Since I'm a college student, I'm interested in apps for learning.

7. **Topic sentence** I think the price is the most important factor I consider when purchasing a smartphone app.

   Time killer I have a few reasons why.

   Reason 1 First of all, I'm a student, and I live on a tight budget, so I can't afford to purchase expensive apps.

   Reason 2 Also, I can purchase many apps if the price of the apps are cheap.

   Wrap up So, I think the price is the most important factor I consider when purchasing a smartphone app.

Translation 해석

상황 설정

호주의 한 기술지가 여러분의 나라에서 어떤 조사를 하고 있다고 가정해 봅시다. 여러분은 스마트폰 앱에 대한 유선 설문 조사에 응했습니다.

5번 질문, 모범 답안

Q: 스마트폰 앱을 마지막으로 사용한 게 언제인가요? 그리고 어떤 앱을 사용했나요?
A: 마지막으로 스마트폰 앱을 사용한 것은 몇 시간 전이고, SNS 앱을 사용했습니다.

6번 질문, 모범 답안

Q: 학습 목적의 앱과 오락 목적의 앱 중 어떤 종류를 주로 구매하시나요? 그 이유는요?
A: 학습 목적의 앱을 주로 구매하는 편입니다. 저는 대학생이기 때문에, 학습용 앱에 관심이 많습니다.

7번 질문, 모범 답안

Q: 다음 중 스마트폰 앱 구매 시 가장 중요하게 생각하는 요소는 무엇입니까? 그 이유는 무엇입니까?
- 가격
- 사용자 친화적인 디자인
- 고품질 고객 지원

A: **Topic sentence** 제가 스마트폰 앱을 구매할 때 가장 중요하게 고려하는 요소는 가격인 것 같습니다.

Time killer 몇 가지 이유가 있습니다.

Reason 1 우선, 저는 학생이고 생활비가 빠듯해서 비싼 앱을 구매할 여유가 없습니다.

Reason 2 또한, 앱의 가격이 저렴하면 여러 앱을 구매할 수 있습니다.

Wrap up 그래서 제가 스마트폰 앱을 구매할 때 가장 중요하게 고려하는 요소는 가격이라고 생각합니다.

PART 4 Respond to questions using information provided

GROUNDWORK

📍 Type Analysis: Resume / Itinerary 유형 분석: 이력서/여행 일정표

Background Knowledge 배경 지식

We will now look at an individual's resume and travel itinerary. Many students study only the schedule type of table to take the test, but it's essential to thoroughly prepare for resume and itinerary types as well, as they can also be included in the test.

이번 단원은 이력서와 여행 일정표를 다루고 있습니다. 많은 수험생들이 일정표 유형만 공부한 뒤 시험에 응시하지만, 이력서 또는 여행 일정표 또한 출제 가능성이 있는 유형이므로 철저히 대비할 필요가 있습니다.

Resume

When you are asked about information on a resume, note that addresses, phone numbers, and e-mail addresses are not usually asked on the test. Also, question 9 will be from the "skills" section over 90% of the time. To respond to the questions, get used to the expressions below, and try to use the correct prepositions:

- work for ~에 근무하다, 다니다
- graduate from ~를 졸업하다
- get one's degree in ~인 전공에서 학위를 취득하다
- work as ~로 근무하다

Itinerary

When it comes to an itinerary, you will probably be asked to explain all the details regarding departure, arrival, transportation, and accommodation. Therefore, the most important thing is the proper and correct use of prepositions.

- be scheduled to depart/leave from ~에서 출발하기로 예정되어 있다
- be scheduled to arrive in/return to ~에 도착하기로 예정되어 있다
- will be staying at/in ~에서 묵을 예정이다
- will take ~를 탈 예정이다

In addition, when reading numbers for the flight or hotel room, refer to the following examples and read the numbers correctly.

- flight 237 flight number two three seven
- hotel room 417 hotel room number four seventeen

Practice 적용 연습

Based on what you have learned, answer the following questions.
학습한 내용을 바탕으로, 다음 질문에 답변해 보세요.

Question

Tim Hill
8807 Tribeca Ave. San Diego, CA 92123
619-885-1109
tim.hill@proco.com

- Desired Position : Chief Product Designer

Employment History	Ace Furniture Company: Furniture designer, 2019~Present
	Trillion Products: Head designer, 2013~2018
Education	University of Greenlake Bachelor's degree: Industrial Design, 2010 Master's degree: Product Development, 2013
Skills and Certificates	Best student design award, 2011 Award for energy-saving design, State Environment Council, 2012

1. What company is he currently working for?
2. I would love to work with someone who is knowledgeable about energy-saving design. Is he fitting?
3. Could you please tell me about his educational background?

Model Answer

1. He is currently working for Ace Furniture Company.
2. Yes, he is. He has received the award for energy-saving design from the state environment council.
3. Sure. He graduated from the University of Greenlake. He got his bachelor's degree in industrial design in 2010 and his master's degree in product development in 2013.

Question

Travel Itinerary for Annan Uba		
Trip to Mombasa Depart Nairobi, Kenya: Royal Airlines, Flight 213 Arrive Mombasa, Kenya	1:45 p.m. 2:50 p.m.	October 7 October 7
Hotel Information: Kings Hotel- Mombasa		October 7-14
Day Trip: Tour of Samburu National Reserve Arrive in Samburu Return to Mombasa	8:00 a.m. 5:30 p.m.	October 10 October 10
Return Trip to Nairobi Depart Mombasa, Royal Airlines, Flight 858 Arrive Nairobi	10:15 a.m. 11:30 a.m.	October 14 October 14

1. What is the name of my hotel in Mombasa, and what dates will I be staying there?
2. I was hoping to go to a festival on October tenth in Mombasa. The festival starts at three p.m. Will I be able to go to that?
3. Can you give me all the details of my return trip to Nairobi, please?

Model Answer

1. The name of the hotel is Kings Hotel, and you will be staying there from October seventh to October fourteenth.
2. Actually, that's not possible. You are scheduled to return to Mombasa at five thirty p.m.
3. Sure. You are scheduled to depart from Mombasa at ten fifteen a.m. and arrive in Nairobi at eleven thirty on October fourteenth. You will take Royal Airlines, flight eight five eight.

MINI TEST

C5 P4 Mini Test

TOEIC Speaking — Question 8-10 of 11

Dorothy McKnight
143 Love St. Lafayette, CA 90823
Tel: 415-663-7572
e-mail: dmck143@palmer.net

- Desired Position : Budget Analyst

Education	Lafayette University - Master's degree in Public Administration (budget & finance), 2018 Contra Costa College - Bachelor's degree in Accounting, 2012
Employment History	Budget Analyst - Lafayette Insurance (2020~present) Accountant - Bell Tech. (2017~2020)
Other skills	Public speaking: previously presented at several conventions Fluent in French

PREPARATION TIME
00:00:45

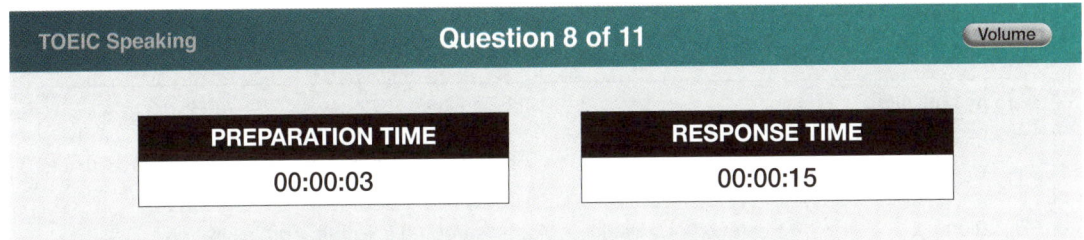

HINT Useful Expression 유용한 표현
- Master's degree 석사 학위
- get one's degree from ~에서 …의 학위를 취득하다
- get one's degree in ~인 전공으로 …의 학위를 취득하다

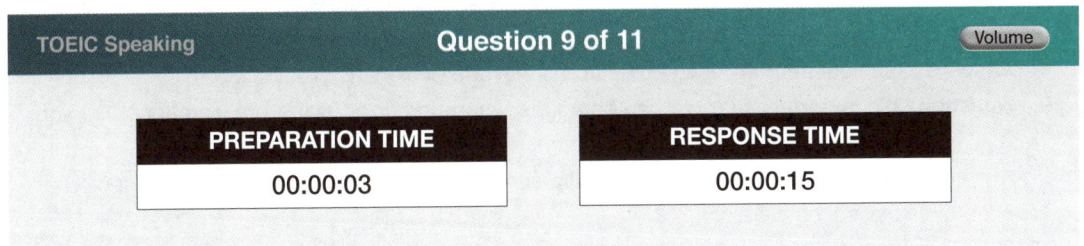

HINT Useful Expression 유용한 표현
- hire 고용하다
- eligible 자격이 있는
- be great at ~에 뛰어난
- public speaking skills 대중 연설 능력
- give presentations 발표하다
- previously 이전에

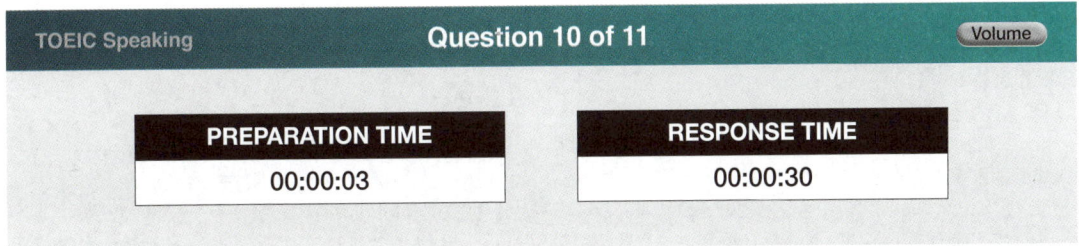

HINT Useful Expression 유용한 표현
- get the details 세부 사항을 알다
- work as ~로 근무하다
- employment history 경력
- accountant 회계사
- work for ~에 근무하다, 다니다
- budget analyst 예산 분석가

Model Answer 모범 답안

🎧 C5 P4 Model Answer

Dorothy McKnight
143 Love St. Lafayette, CA 90823

Tel: 415-663-7572
e-mail: dmck143@palmer.net

- Desired Position : Budget Analyst

Education	❽ Lafayette University - Master's degree in Public Administration (budget & finance), 2018 Contra Costa College - Bachelor's degree in Accounting, 2012
❿ Employment History	Budget Analyst - Lafayette Insurance (2020~present) Accountant - Bell Tech. (2017~2020)
Other skills	❾ Public speaking: previously presented at several conventions Fluent in French

Narration: Hi, this is Katrina Evans. I have an interview with Dorothy McKnight, but it seems that I've misplaced her resume. I hope you could give me some information I need.

8. Question: Where did Ms. McKnight get her Master's degree?
Answer: She got her master's degree from Lafayette University.

9. Question: It's important that we hire someone who is great at giving presentations. Do you think she is eligible?
Answer: Yes, she is. She has good public speaking skills. She has previously presented at several conventions.

10. Question: I would like to get all the details about Ms. McKnight's previous employment history. Can you tell me about the companies she has worked for?
Answer: Sure. She worked as an accountant at Bell Tech. from 2017 to 2020. She has been working as a budget analyst at Lafayette Insurance since 2020.

Translation 해석

나레이션
안녕하세요. Katrina Evans입니다. Dorothy McKnight 씨와 면접이 있는데요. 그분의 이력서를 어디에 뒀는지 잊은 것 같아요. 몇 가지 정보를 좀 알려주실 수 있을까요?

8번 질문, 모범 답안
Q: McKnight 씨는 어디에서 석사 학위를 받았습니까?
A: 그녀는 Lafayette University에서 석사 학위를 받았습니다.

9번 질문, 모범 답안
Q: 발표를 잘하는 사람을 고용하는 것이 중요합니다. 그녀가 자질이 있다고 생각하십니까?
A: 예, 그렇습니다. 그녀는 훌륭한 대중 연설 능력을 가지고 있습니다. 그녀는 이전에 여러 대규모 회의에서 발표를 한 적이 있습니다.

10번 질문, 모범 답안
Q: McKnight 씨의 이전 직장에 대한 세부 정보를 알고 싶습니다. 그녀가 근무했던 회사에 대해 알려주실 수 있으십니까?
A: 물론이죠. 그녀는 Bell Tech.에서 2017년부터 2020년까지 회계사로 일했습니다. 그리고 2020년부터 현재까지는 Lafayette Insurance에서 예산 분석가로 일하고 있습니다.

PART 5 Express an opinion

GROUNDWORK

📍 Master The Basics 이론 학습

Background Knowledge 배경 지식

Introducing an additional idea pattern that you can apply in PART 5. If it is challenging to form your answer centered around "the Internet," you can also consider utilizing "work" as a subject of your answer.

PART 5에서 활용할 수 있는 또 다른 아이디어 패턴을 소개합니다. '인터넷'을 소재로 답변을 풀어 나가기 어렵다면, '업무'를 소재로 답변을 이어 나갈 수 있습니다.

Useful Idea Pattern : W-pattern

The "W" stands for "Work". This pattern will help you answer questions that are related to work, work skills, jobs, business, and education, which are very likely to be presented on the test.

Idea Pattern Examples

- I think it is one of the best ways to maximize your work potential.
  저는 그것이 자신의 업무 잠재력을 최대치로 끌어올릴 수 있는 가장 좋은 방법 중 하나라고 생각합니다.

- I believe that work efficiency and productivity can be increased by _____.
  _____을 통해서 업무의 능률과 생산성이 증진될 수 있다고 생각합니다.

- It leads to high work performance.
  이는 높은 업무 성과로 이어집니다.

- _____ will have a positive impact on a person's work performance and assist them in overcoming various challenges.
  _____은 일에 긍정적인 영향을 주고 여러 도전적인 상황을 극복할 수 있도록 도와줄 것입니다.

- _____ can accomplish more and expect great outcomes by _____.
  _____는 _____을 통해 성취도를 높이고 훌륭한 결과를 기대할 수 있습니다.

How to Apply

Question:

Do you agree or disagree with the following statement?

An effective business leader must have good negotiating skills.

Give specific reasons or examples to support your opinion.

Answer:

I agree with the statement that an effective business leader must have good negotiating skills. I think negotiating skills are an important part of running a business. It could have a lot of benefits. I believe that business efficiency can be increased by good negotiating skills. If someone has good negotiating skills, they can steer negotiations in favor of their business which leads to high business performance. Having good negotiating skills will have a positive impact on the business and assist it in overcoming various challenges. A leader can accomplish more and expect great outcomes by having good negotiating skills. Therefore, I definitely agree with the statement that an effective business leader must have good negotiating skills.

Practice 적용 연습

Based on what you have learned, answer the following questions.
학습한 내용을 바탕으로, 다음 질문에 답변해 보세요.

Question

Do you agree or disagree with the following statement?

Watching TV has a negative effect on teenagers.

Give specific reasons or examples to support your opinion.

Apply the Idea Pattern

I disagree with the statement that watching TV has a negative effect on teenagers. I think watching TV has a positive impact on teenager's education. It can be beneficial. I believe that their productivity can be increased by **1.** _____. Allowing them to engage in activities they enjoy will ultimately have **2.** _____ on their ability to concentrate on their studies. After fulfilling their leisure pursuits, they are more likely to focus on their academic tasks, leading to **3.** _____. Therefore, I definitely agree that watching TV has a **4.** _____ on teenagers.

Model Answer

1. watching TV
2. a positive impact
3. high concentration
4. positive effect

MINI TEST

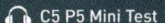

C5 P5 Mini Test

TOEIC Speaking Question 11 of 11 Volume

What are the benefits of doing an internship before graduating from university? Give specific reasons or examples to support your answer.

PREPARATION TIME	RESPONSE TIME
00:00:45	00:00:60

Model Answer 모범 답안

🎧 C5 P5 Model Answer

I believe there are many advantages to doing an internship before graduating from university. **It is one of the best ways to maximize your work potential.** I am of the opinion that **your work efficiency and productivity can be enhanced by experiencing the work process.** Once your work efficiency and productivity have been enhanced through an internship, your work ability will be competitive enough in the job market, making it easier to get a job after graduation. Furthermore, even after securing a job, **the internship experience will continue to have a positive impact on your work and assist you in overcoming various challenges. You can accomplish more and expect great outcomes by reflecting on your internship experience.** These are the advantages to doing an internship before graduating from university.

Translation 해석

문제
대학생들이 졸업하기 전에 인턴십을 하면 어떤 이점이 있나요?
구체적인 근거와 사례를 들어 의견을 뒷받침하십시오.

모범 답안
저는 대학 졸업 전 인턴십을 하는 것에 많은 이점이 있다고 생각합니다. **인턴십을 하는 것은 업무 잠재력을 극대화하는 가장 좋은 방법 중 하나입니다.** 제 의견은, **업무 과정을 경험함으로써 업무 효율성과 생산성이 향상될 수 있다는 것입니다.** 인턴십을 통해 업무 효율성과 생산성이 향상되면, 취업 시장에서 충분히 경쟁력 있는 업무 역량을 갖추게 될 것이고, 이는 졸업 후 취업을 더욱 수월하게 만들어 줄 것입니다. 그뿐만 아니라, **인턴십 경험은 취업 후에도 계속해서 업무에 긍정적인 영향을 미치며 다양한 어려움을 극복하는 데 도움이 될 것입니다. 인턴십 경험을 떠올리며 더 많은 것을 성취하고 훌륭한 성과를 기대할 수 있기 때문입니다.** 이러한 것들이 대학 졸업 전 인턴십을 하는 것의 이점입니다.

REVIEW TEST 5

TOEIC Speaking — **Question 1 of 11** — Volume

Welcome to the Grossmont Film Festival. We'll begin screening our opening film in a few minutes. But first, it's my honor to introduce this year's special guest, Veronica Wheeler. Ms. Wheeler has brought creativity, skills, and experience to the film industry throughout her career. It's certain she would be an excellent addition to the judging panel tonight.

PREPARATION TIME	RESPONSE TIME
00:00:45	00:00:45

TOEIC Speaking — **Question 2 of 11** — Volume

In just a moment, we will welcome a well-known real estate expert, Bill Stanford, to the studio. Mr. Stanford will be talking about locating the hottest areas, budgeting money, and making correct investment plans. At the end of the show, he will also be taking questions from the audience. Let's welcome Bill Stanford to the studio!

PREPARATION TIME	RESPONSE TIME
00:00:45	00:00:45

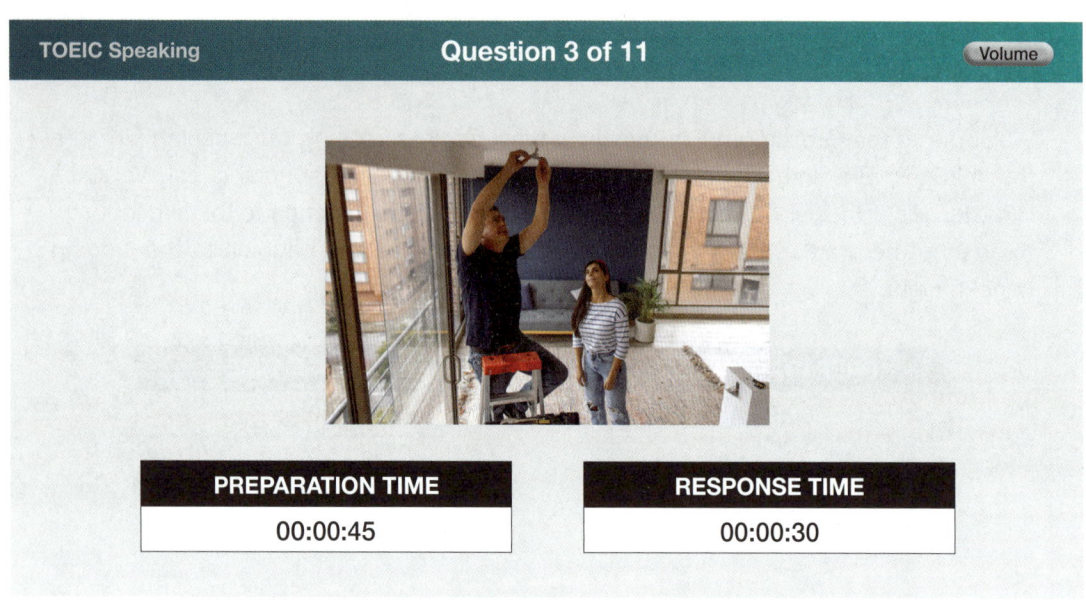

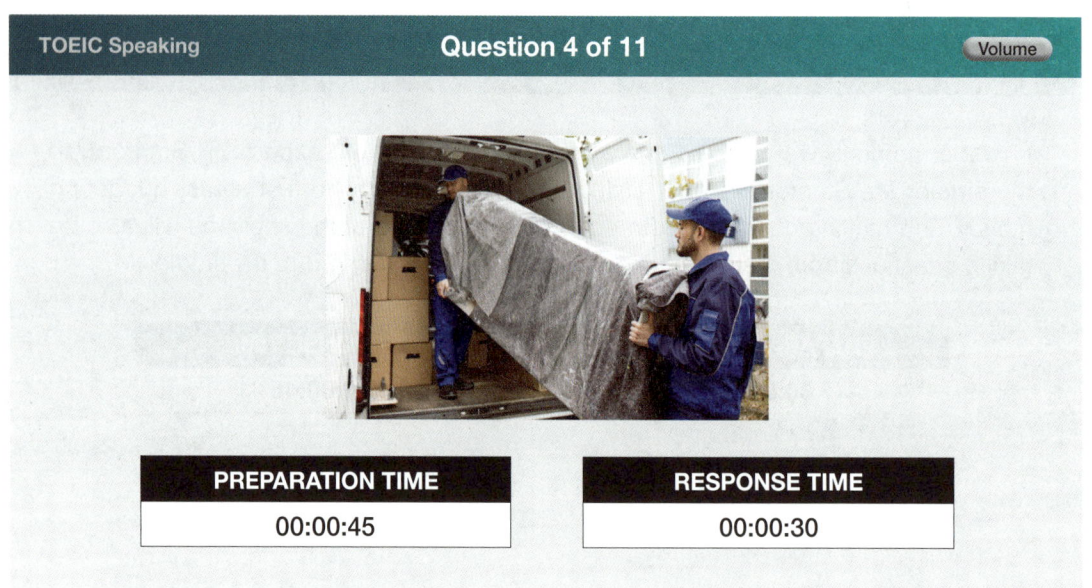

| TOEIC Speaking | Question 5 of 11 | |

Imagine that a Canadian interior design company is doing research in your country. You have agreed to participate in a telephone interview about buying furniture.

When was the last time you bought a piece of furniture, and what did you buy?

PREPARATION TIME	RESPONSE TIME
00:00:03	00:00:15

| TOEIC Speaking | Question 6 of 11 | |

Imagine that a Canadian interior design company is doing research in your country. You have agreed to participate in a telephone interview about buying furniture.

Do you change your furniture often? Why or why not?

PREPARATION TIME	RESPONSE TIME
00:00:03	00:00:15

| TOEIC Speaking | Question 7 of 11 | |

Imagine that a Canadian interior design company is doing research in your country. You have agreed to participate in a telephone interview about buying furniture.

Besides price, what is the most important factor when you buy furniture? Why?

PREPARATION TIME	RESPONSE TIME
00:00:03	00:00:30

Business Travel for Jessica Milton

Information	Date and Time
<Flight Information> Depart: Boston, P-Way Airline flight #302 Arrive: Dublin (*The rental car is reserved at the airport.*)	Aug. 20, 9:30 a.m. Aug. 20, 9:30 p.m.
Depart: Dublin, P-Way Airline flight #124 Arrive: Boston	Aug. 27, 5:00 p.m. Aug. 27, 9:15 p.m.
<Hotel Information> Richardson Hotel in Dublin	Aug. 20 ~ Aug. 27
<Day Trip Information> • Factory in Shankill • Howth headquarters	Aug. 22, 10:00 a.m. ~ 2:00 p.m. Aug. 25, 8:00 a.m. ~ Noon

PREPARATION TIME
00:00:45

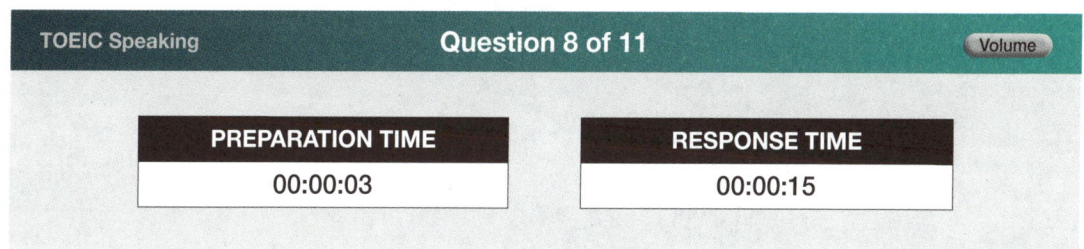

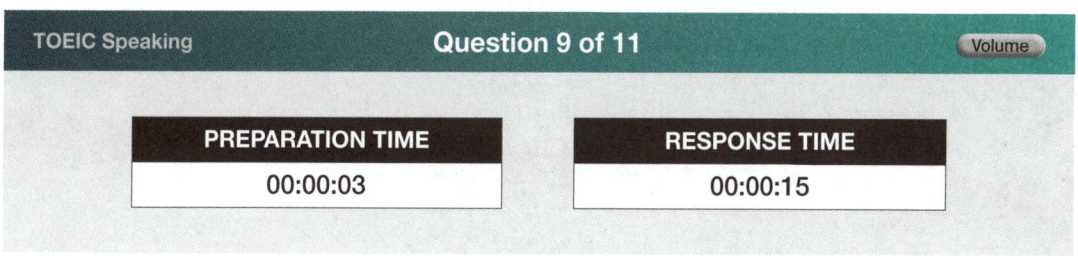

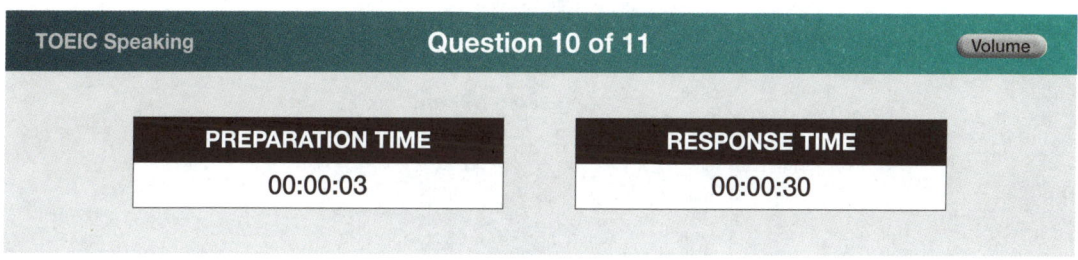

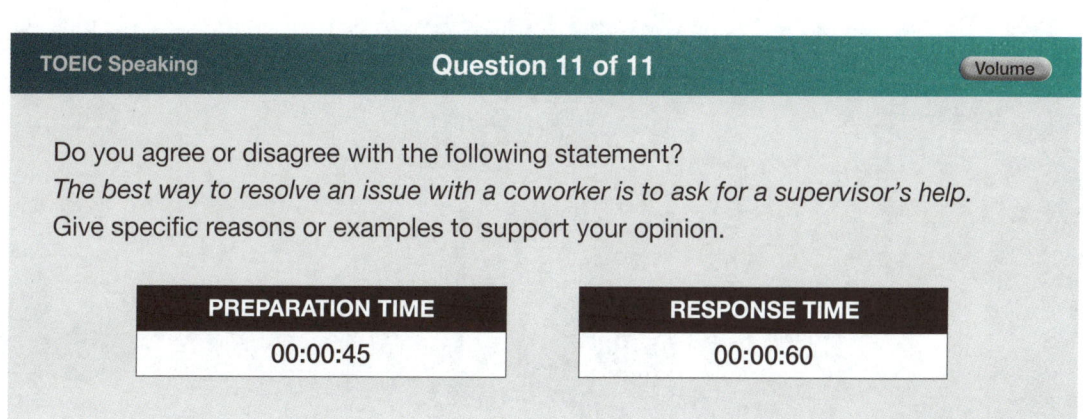

Do you agree or disagree with the following statement?
The best way to resolve an issue with a coworker is to ask for a supervisor's help.
Give specific reasons or examples to support your opinion.

Actual Test

ACTUAL TEST 1

TOEIC Speaking — Question 1 of 11 — Volume

When you need new shoes for any occasion, Splash Footwear is here for you. We've been in business for over four years, serving customers from all over the Coronado area. This Sunday, we're having unbelievable sales on sneakers, beach sandals, and much more. Don't miss this amazing opportunity to find the perfect footwear for you.

PREPARATION TIME	RESPONSE TIME
00:00:45	00:00:45

TOEIC Speaking — Question 2 of 11 — Volume

Welcome, listeners, to Radio Eleven's interview of the week. On today's broadcast, we have a successful business man and marvelous writer, Danny Min. Min's book, *Thirty Hours a Day*, provides helpful tips and advice on time management. Topics include managing workloads, meeting deadlines, and making the most of your free time. For millions of readers, it has become the most beloved book of the year.

PREPARATION TIME	RESPONSE TIME
00:00:45	00:00:45

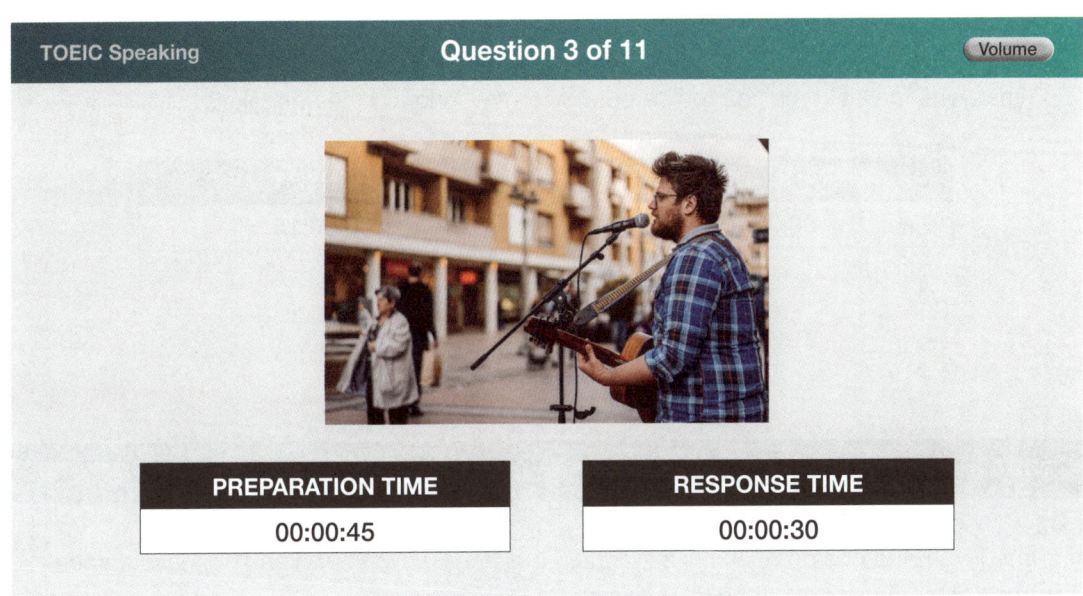

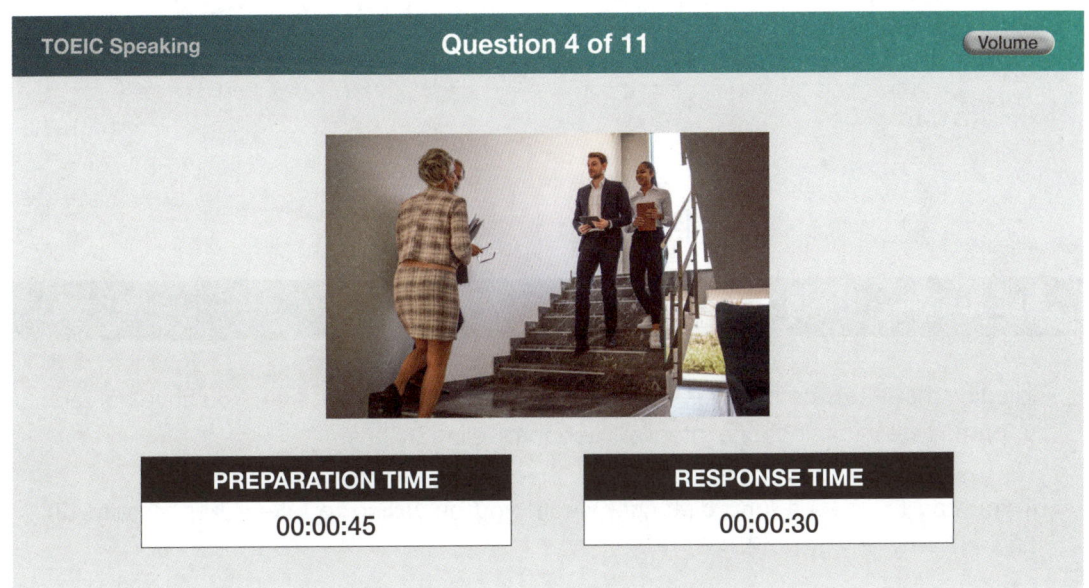

| TOEIC Speaking | Question 5 of 11 | |

Imagine that a bus company is expanding bus services in your area. You have agreed to participate in a telephone interview about traveling by bus.

When was the last time you took a bus? And how long did the ride take?

PREPARATION TIME	RESPONSE TIME
00:00:03	00:00:15

| TOEIC Speaking | Question 6 of 11 | |

Imagine that a bus company is expanding bus services in your area. You have agreed to participate in a telephone interview about traveling by bus.

Do you think the bus service in your area is easy to use? Why or why not?

PREPARATION TIME	RESPONSE TIME
00:00:03	00:00:15

| TOEIC Speaking | Question 7 of 11 | |

Imagine that a bus company is expanding bus services in your area. You have agreed to participate in a telephone interview about traveling by bus.

If you had to travel a long distance, would you be willing to take a bus instead of driving? Why or why not?

PREPARATION TIME	RESPONSE TIME
00:00:03	00:00:30

Actingtowne
December Class Schedule
$45/session

DATE	TIME	CLASS	NOTE
Dec. 3	2:00 p.m. ~ 6:00 p.m.	Introduction to Acting	Textbook: Basics of Acting
Dec. 11	3:00 p.m. ~ 5:30 p.m.	Lecture: Stage Techniques	Speaker: Pat Damon
Dec. 15	5:00 p.m. ~ 7:00 p.m.	Demonstration: Improvisation Techniques	Speaker: Jackson Black
Dec. 22	9:00 a.m. ~ 3:00 p.m.	Acting Camp	Boxed lunch provided
Dec. 28	2:30 p.m. ~ 4:00 p.m.	Lecture: Finding an Agent	Speaker: Gillian Williamson
Dec. 30	4:00 p.m. ~ 6:00 p.m.	The Final Touch of Acting	Speaker: George Clubbs

PREPARATION TIME
00:00:45

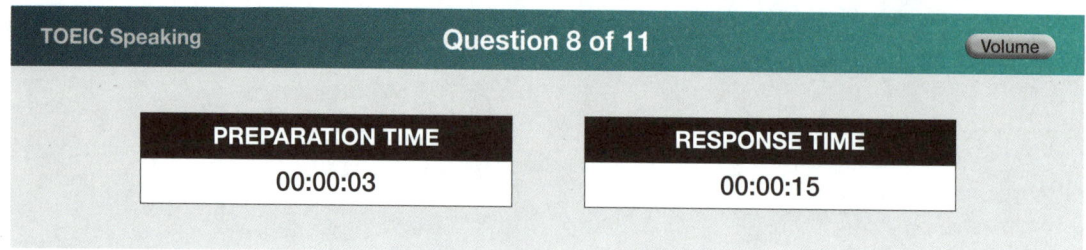

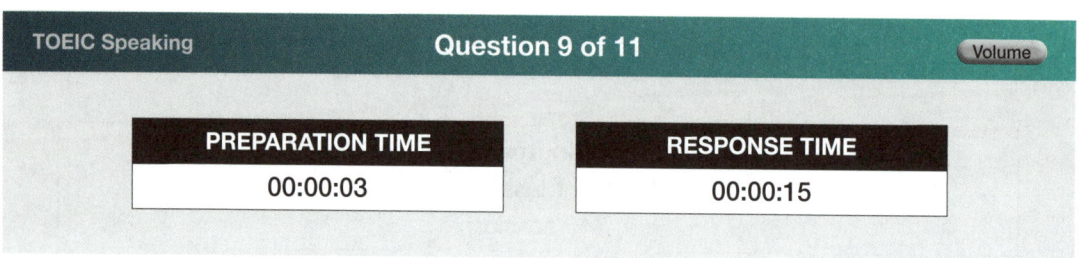

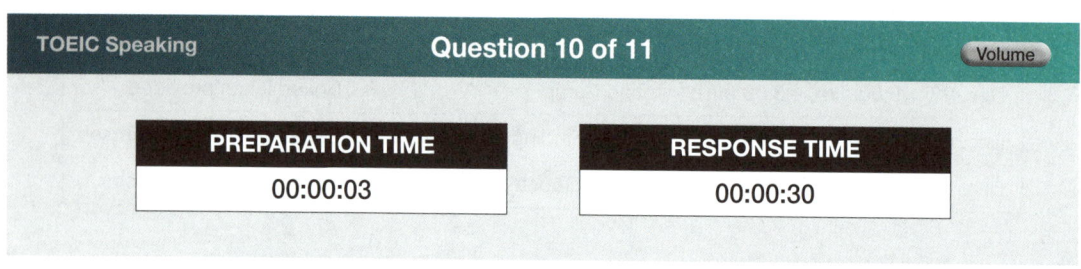

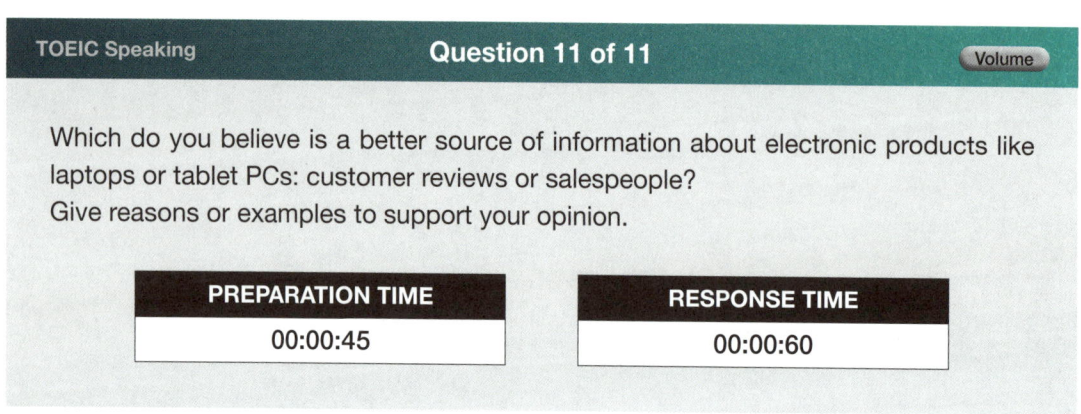

Which do you believe is a better source of information about electronic products like laptops or tablet PCs: customer reviews or salespeople?
Give reasons or examples to support your opinion.

ACTUAL TEST 2

TOEIC Speaking Question 1 of 11

Welcome to the Point Loma Harbor Cruise! Our nightly tour provides scenic views of bridges, buildings, and other special National City landmarks. In fact, the only way to fully experience these many landmarks is from the water! When the cruise begins, have your cameras ready to capture National City's treasures.

PREPARATION TIME	RESPONSE TIME
00:00:45	00:00:45

TOEIC Speaking Question 2 of 11

Ladies and gentlemen, we appreciate your attendance at this fundraiser, which benefits the local youth football team. Thanks to your generosity, more children can participate in sports. Through sports, children can learn teamwork, discipline, and fairness. Now, if you turn towards the screen, you will see a short video that the football team has prepared for you.

PREPARATION TIME	RESPONSE TIME
00:00:45	00:00:45

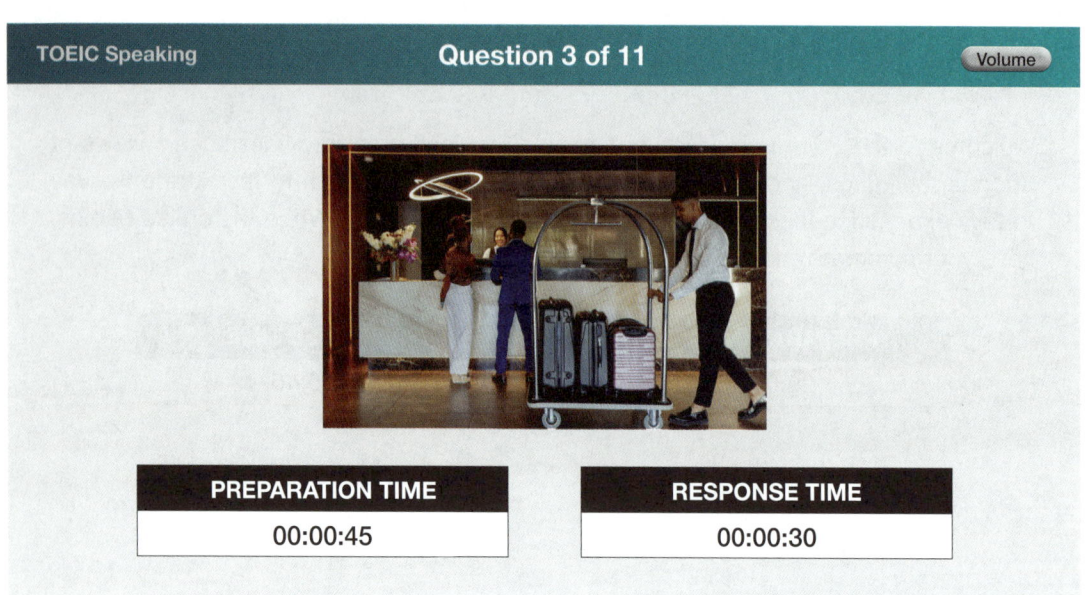

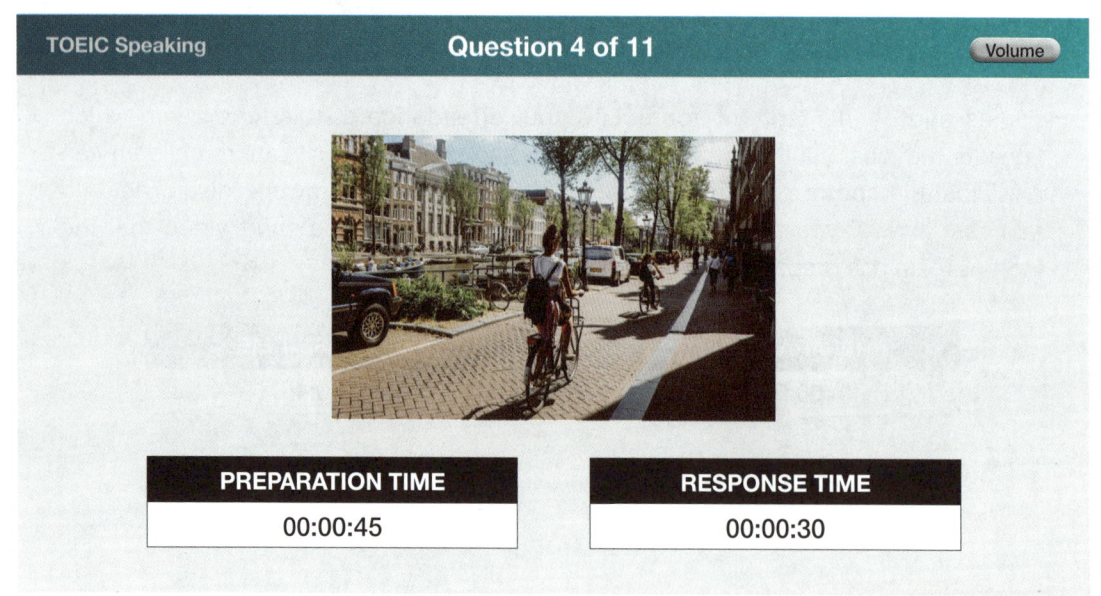

TOEIC Speaking — Question 5 of 11

Imagine that a local library is doing research in your area. You have agreed to participate in a telephone interview about having book discussion groups.

How long should a book discussion last? Why?

PREPARATION TIME	RESPONSE TIME
00:00:03	00:00:15

TOEIC Speaking — Question 6 of 11

Imagine that a local library is doing research in your area. You have agreed to participate in a telephone interview about having book discussion groups.

Do you think having book discussion groups would help children and teens? Why?

PREPARATION TIME	RESPONSE TIME
00:00:03	00:00:15

TOEIC Speaking — Question 7 of 11

Imagine that a local library is doing research in your area. You have agreed to participate in a telephone interview about having book discussion groups.

Which of the following would be most interesting to read in a book discussion group? Why?
- Novels
- Poems
- Classics

PREPARATION TIME	RESPONSE TIME
00:00:03	00:00:30

TOEIC Speaking Question 8-10 of 11

Triumph Business Center
Professional Management Training Seminar
Daily rate: $40 / 2-Day rate: $70

Feb. 14	
10:00 a.m.	Keynote Speech: Effective Management (Nicole Stewart)
11:00 a.m.	Lecture: Improving Communication (Ronda Harper)
Noon	Lunch
~~12:30 p.m.~~	~~Lecture: Software Tools for Better Management (Frank Dorson)~~ Canceled
1:30 p.m.	Workshop: Helping Employees Advance (James Naomi)
Feb. 15	
9:45 a.m.	Lecture: Collaboration Between Departments (Lucas Clover)
11:00 a.m.	Workshop: The Right Way to Resolve Issues Between Employees (Oliver Nelson)
Noon	Lunch
1:00 p.m.	Video: Situational Leadership for Managers

PREPARATION TIME
00:00:45

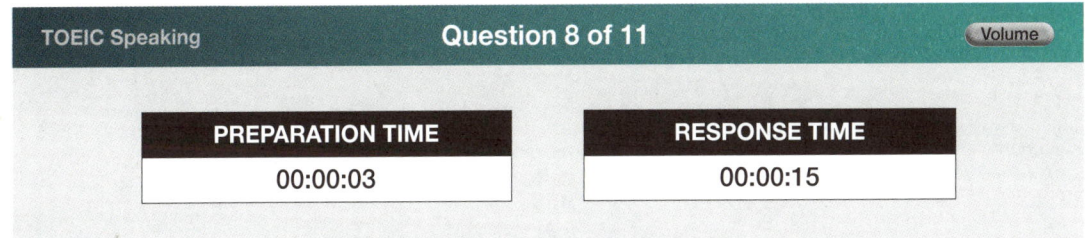

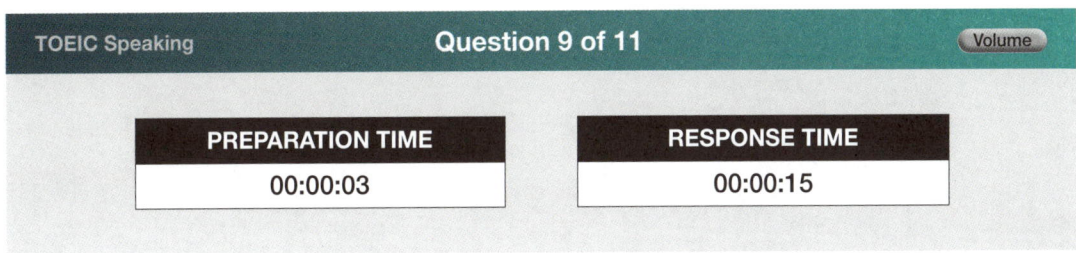

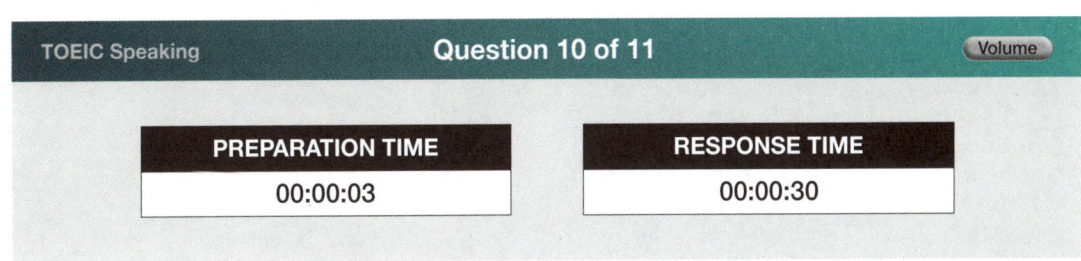

Do you agree or disagree with the following statement?
It is necessary to give up time with friends and family in order to achieve one's professional goals.
Give reasons or examples to support your opinion.

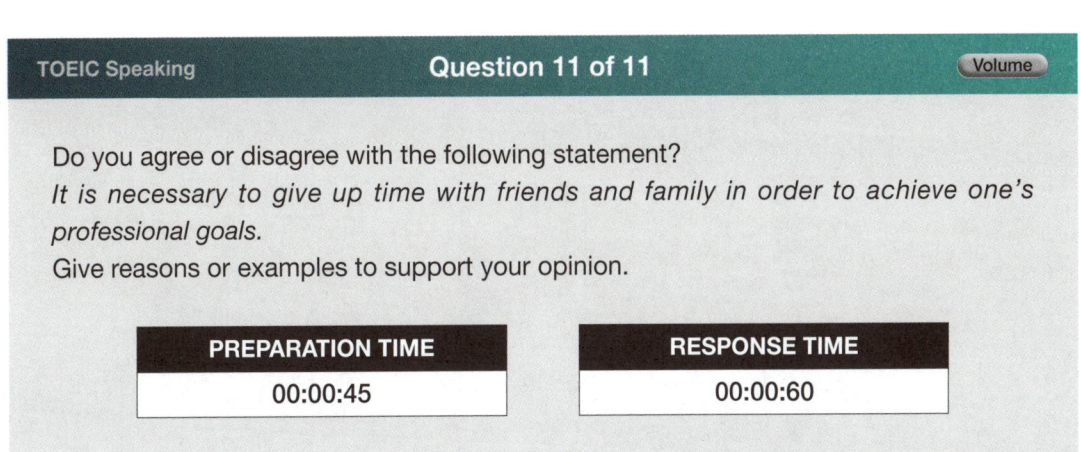

Memo